FLAMING OLYMPICS

Illustrated by
Aidan Potts and Mike Phillips

To Stephen and Matthew

Scholastic Children's Books,
Euston House, 24 Eversholt Street,
London NW1 1DB, UK

A division of Scholastic Ltd
London ~ New York ~ Toronto ~ Sydney ~ Auckland
Mexico City ~ New Delhi ~ Hong Kong

Flaming Olympics
First published in the UK by Scholastic Ltd, 1996
Text © Michael Coleman, 1996, 2004, 2008, 2012, 2016
Illustrations © Aidan Potts, 1996
Updated illustrations © Mike Phillips, 2004, 2008, 2012, 2016

Flaming Olympics Quiz Book
First published in the UK by Scholastic Ltd, 2004
Text © Michael Coleman, 2004, 2012, 2016
Illustrations © Mike Phillips, 2004, 2012, 2016

This edition published 2016

ISBN 978 1407 16397 0

Printed and bound by CPI Group (UK) Ltd, Croydon, CR0 4YY

2 4 6 8 10 9 7 5 3 1

The right of Michael Coleman, Aidan Potts and Mike Phillips to be
identified as the author and illustrators of this work respectively has
been asserted by them in accordance with the Copyright, Designs and
Patents Act, 1988.

Papers used by Scholastic Children's Books are made from woods
grown in sustainable forests.

FLAMING OLYMPICS
CONTENTS

INTRODUCTION: WELCOME TO RIO!

From the 5th to the 21st of August 2016 the Summer Olympic Games are being held in Rio de Janeiro, Brazil – a modern version of a competition which began in 776 BC!

The Olympic Games are held every four years in a different city. Since the modern version of the Summer Olympics began in 1896 (you'll find out all about the ancient version later in this book) they've been all round the world – but 2016 will be the first time they've been on the road to Rio. The people of Brazil are promising a rio(tous) Games!

So – why do you think this book has been called *Flaming Olympics*? Is it because:
• Rio's temperatures are going to be red-hot?
• Running tracks used to be made out of cinders?
• Lots of races are held in heats?
• The man who started the Olympics was a bright spark?

Sorry, if you've picked one of these, you're wrong!
    Here are another four to choose from. Is this book called *Flaming Olympics* because:
• There've been loads of scorching performances at the Olympics?

5

- There've been plenty of red faces at the Olympics?
- There've been lots of flashy characters at the Olympics?
- There've been dozens of blazing rows at the Olympics?

You've said "yes" to one of these? Now, you're getting warmer! Over the years there have been loads of red-hot performances, red faces, flashy characters and blazing rows!

But none of these reasons are exactly why the book's called *Flaming Olympics*. So why is it? Check out the word 'flame' in your dictionary. You'll discover that one of its meanings is something like: *to become violently excited, passionate or angry*.

That's why this book is called *Flaming Olympics*. It's because, of all the sporting occasions in the world, none has seen as many exciting, or passionate, or angry incidents take place as the Olympic Games. In fact there've been so many amazing incidents over the years it's a wonder the Olympic Games haven't been renamed the Olympic Fun and Games! In this book you'll not only read about the best incidents but also learn some odd Olympic things with our special 'Flaming Facts'.

So, if you want to amaze your friends and wow your teachers with tales of:
- Flaming Olympic champs and chumps
- Flaming Olympic tracks and tricks
- Flaming Olympic disputes and disasters...

... then read on!

THE FLAMING ANCIENT OLYMPICS

The Olympic Games aren't a new invention, you know. They've been around for well over 2,500 years – that's probably even before your teacher was born (although you might like to check to make sure)! They were first held in the Kingdom of Elis, in Greece, at a site called Olympia – which is how the word *Olympic* came to be used. (Check out your atlas – these places still exist.)

There's a powerful legend about how the Games began. It's said that they were the invention of a Greek hero called Heracles...

Heracles' big job

Now Heracles, or Hercules as he became more commonly known, was a sort of Greek version of Superman. He was supposed to be the son of Zeus, the Greek god in charge of thunder and lightning – a flaming Greek god if ever there was one! This might explain why Heracles was always having flashes of temper! One of his earliest occurred during a music lesson. Heracles objected to being told by his teacher, Linus,

IS IT A BIRD? IS IT A PLANE? NO! IT'S **HERACLES !!!**

that his lyre-playing wasn't very good. So, what did he do? He swung his lyre and killed his teacher with one blow. (Was this pop music's first number one hit?)

After that, Heracles went on to kill a few other creatures – including a lion – until one day he killed some of his own children. This made the gods pretty angry and, although Heracles said he was sorry, they decided that wasn't enough.

Heracles was given twelve jobs to carry out as a punishment, a sort of super-detention. These jobs became known as the Twelve Labours of Heracles. One of them was for the King of Augea.

Heracles put on his best suit and turned up on time. He soon realized that putting on his best suit had been a bad move. The conversation went something like this…

How king-sized was Heracles' problem? Can you do the sums?

3,000 oxen, doing 2 poos per day

= _____ ox-poos per day

x 365 (for every day in the year, but ignoring leap years)

= _____ ox-poos per year

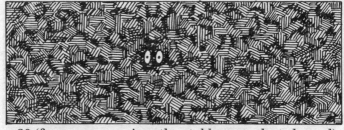

x 30 (for every year since the stables were last cleaned)

= _____ ox-poos all together!

But Heracles managed it. How? Simple. Instead of messing about with a mop and bucket, he used his superpowers to change the direction of two rivers so that they flowed right through the stables and out the other side. The water swept all before it (I'd hate to think where!), and the stables were cleaned.

And, so the story goes, 'flushed' with success at how strong and quick he'd been, Heracles decided to celebrate by setting up a competition in which everybody else could see how strong and quick they were. He called this competition the Olympic Games, and dedicated them in honour of his father, Zeus.

Flaming festivals

However they really came about, the ancient Games were first and foremost a religious festival. That is, as well as the different sporting competitions, there was a lot of praying and sacrificing going on in honour of good old Zeus.

At first this just took one day. Then more events were added and they needed two days. Then more and more events were added, so that by 692 BC the Olympics were lasting a full five days.

So, what went on? Here's an early programme (bought from an early programme-seller – yes, they had those, too).

OLYMPIC GAMES

TO BE HELD AT OLYMPIA IN THE KINGDOM OF ELIS
FOR THE HONOUR OF ZEUS

DAY 1
OPENING PROCESSION AND SACRIFICES TO ZEUS.
JUDGES' SWEARING AND ATHLETES' OATHS.
(BUT BAD LANGUAGE FROM SPECTATORS WILL NOT BE TOLERATED.)

DAY 2
PENTATHLON·
POETRY AND ALL THAT CISSY STUFF·
CHARIOT RACES·

DAY 3
MORE SACRIFICES TO ZEUS·
FOOT-RACES·

DAY 4
RUNNING·IN·ARMOUR RACE · BOXING·
WRESTLING · PANKRATION ·
(NOTE: SPECTATORS CAUGHT FIGHTING
WILL BE THROWN OUT·)

DAY 5
PRIZE-GIVING·
THANKSGIVING TO ZEUS·
BANQUET FOR THE WINNERS·

13

...ses, promises

...y, the athletes all swore an oath
...would play fairly.

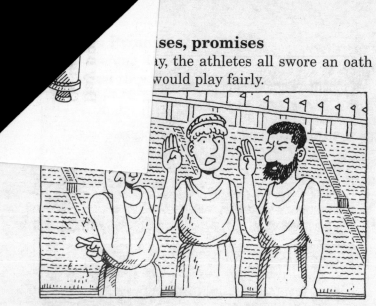

The judges did the same, promising also that they would keep secret anything they learned about a competitor. (Unless they'd found out he'd been cheating! Then they had him whipped.)

Day two: Fun and games

The sporting events started on day two. A five-activity event came first. This was known as the pentathlon, from the Greek word *pente*, meaning 'five'. In the pentathlon competitors had to throw the discus, throw the javelin, run, wrestle and jump – though not all at once of course.

WATCH IT, MATE,
OR I'LL GIVE YOU
A BUNCH OF PENTES!

The chariot races took place on the same day. They could be really gruesome. In every race you would see whips smacking against sweating flesh and hear the awful cries of creatures in agony – and that was just what the chariot drivers were doing to each other! The poor old horses had an even tougher time.

But even they didn't have as tough a time as the oxen on day three...

Day three, morning: Noughts and oxen

If you were going to take part in the ancient Games it was definitely NOT a good idea to be an ox. Why not?

- Because at the start of day three at every Olympiad, you and 99 other oxen would be slaughtered in honour of Zeus.
- You would then be cut up and your thighs burnt to ashes on the altar of Zeus as a sacrifice. (Over the years, this pile of ash grew to 6 metres: not quite sky-high but definitely thigh-high!)
- The rest of you would be eaten by the winning athletes at the big banquet which ended the Games.

Day three, afternoon: Oh, my foot!

After the oxo-cubing, it was time for the foot races. The shortest was the Stade, a straight race down the length of the arena – or 'stadium' – as it came to be known because of its length. A stade measured the curious distance of 192.27 metres. Legends say that this measurement was also based on a supposed fact about Heracles. Was it:

- 60 times the length of Heracles' foot?
- The distance Heracles could walk in one breath?
- The distance Heracles could run in one breath?

Answer: There are legends suggesting all three. (Could they all be right? Maybe Heracles walked by putting one foot in front of the other, and because he was a bit of a thicko, he held his breath because he couldn't do two things at once, but because he was also a super-hero he did it so quickly the groundsman thought he was running...)

There were two other foot races: the *Diaulos* (of two stades, to the end of the stadium and back) and the *Dolichos* (of 24 stades). If you managed to win all

three of these races you were given the title *Triastes*,
meaning 'triple winner'. One fabulous runner named
Leonidas of Rhodes won this title four Games in a
row (or should that be four Games running!).

Day four: Perilous pankration

Day four was not for the faint-hearted. Basically, it
was punch-up day with wrestling and boxing leading
up to the meanest, nastiest, toughest sport ever
invented: *pankration*.

Pankration is a Greek word which is made from
two other Greek words: *pan*, meaning 'all', and
kratew meaning 'be strong, take hold'.

So, what does *pankration* mean? 'Strongest of all'?
'Take hold of everything'? From the sound of what
went on, both of them! Pankration was certainly an
event for the strongest men. But it was also one in
which you were allowed to grab hold of everything
– and, as the fighters were naked, everything was
definitely grabbable!

THAT WAS MY
'BELOW THE BELLY-
BUTTON' SPECIAL!

That's it. In pankration you could do what you liked to your opponent except bite him or put your thumb in his eye and pull it out (your thumb *and* his eye). The trouble was, of course, your opponent could do the same to you! Also, unlike wrestling and boxing nowadays, light and heavy fighters weren't separated. They were put in against each other (which was when the light ones *did* get separated – usually from their arms and legs). There were no rounds, either, for the fighters to take a breather. A pankration match just went on and on until somebody gave in, or dropped – dead if necessary.

Day five: Prize-giving day

For those who survived to see it, day five of the ancient Games was one of celebration. A bit like a school Awards Assembly, this was the day when the prizes were given out to the winners of the different events.

And what were the prizes? At the Games themselves, not much. Just an olive wreath and, if

18

you were brilliantly successful, the honour of having the Games named after you. Apart from that, most of the athletes waited until they got home before they cashed in. Olympic champions would often be given money and good jobs, not asked to pay taxes – even be allowed to eat out free for life.

Flaming Fact

When the Olympics returned to Greece in 2004, every medal winner was given an olive wreath along with their medal. The wreathes for the marathon winners, however, were going to be special. They were going to come from the oldest tree in Greece. Unfortunately there were two contenders, from different villages. Both claimed their tree dated back to the time of the ancient Olympics ... but, unsurprisingly, neither of them was willing to cut it down and count the growth rings to prove it! In the end the wreath for the winner of the women's marathon was made from one tree and that for the men's gold medallist from the other.

Could you have been a judge at the ancient Olympics?

At the ancient Olympics, judges had to be dead honest – otherwise they were likely to end up dead. See how you would have got on in this ancient Olympic quiz.

1. At the opening ceremony, you promise to be an honest judge. How do you show this?
a) By signing an agreement.

b) By saying you'll fall on your sword if you're not honest.

c) By dipping your hands in blood.

2. You've got to make sure all the runners in the foot race start from the same place. What do you do?

a) Scratch a line on the ground and make them stand behind it.

b) Stand in front of them, then get out of the way fast.

c) Hold a javelin out in front of them until they get the point.

3. In the pankration event (a mixture of boxing and wrestling), one man turns up with his fists bound in leather and covered in metal. What do you do?

a) Disqualify him.

b) Tell him to be a good boy and take it all off.

c) Let the fight go on.

4. It's the big pankration final: Aggroppo the 'Ard versus Mangulon the Mad. Aggroppo grabs Mangulon's foot and twists it. Mangulon decides to have a go at strangling him.

Aggroppo twists Mangulon's foot a lot 'arder. But,

just as Mangulon raises one arm to give in, he manages to finish strangling Aggroppo with his other arm. Aggroppo drops down dead. What do you do?

a) Declare Mangulon the winner.

b) Declare Aggroppo the winner.

c) Declare it a draw, but say in your report that Aggroppo was dead unlucky.

5. At the end of a running race it looks like a dead heat between Nippylon and Whippylon. Who gets the victor's laurel wreath?

a) You give them half each.

b) You award it to the god, Zeus.

c) You make them run again.

6. The chariot race comes to a spine-tingling finish with ace driver Hamiltonion just crossing the line first. Who do you award the winner's wreath to?

a) Hamiltonion's horse.

b) Hamiltonion.

c) The owner of Hamiltonion's horse.

7. A runner is guilty of a false start. What do you do?
a) Have him flogged.
b) Make him go back five paces.
c) Disqualify him if he does it again.

8. Women aren't allowed into the Games, but you discover one watching from behind a pillar. What do you do?
a) Have her thrown out.
b) Have her thrown in jail.
c) Have her thrown over the nearest cliff.

Answers:

1. c) Ugh! The blood came from the animals sacrificed to Zeus and was taken to be holy.

2. a) This is how the saying "starting from scratch" came about.

3. c) Let the fight go on. This is how it was in pankration. If the other fighter hadn't been dressed the same, then he wouldn't have stood much chance!

4. b) The loser was the one who gave in. Mangulion did, Aggroppo didn't (and never would, of course).

5. b) A pretty good deal for Zeus, who got a victor's wreath without even putting his shorts on.

6. c) All poor old Hamiltonion would have got was a piece of ribbon.

7. a) As you can imagine, there weren't too many false starts in the ancient Games.

8. c) What's more, the distance she travelled didn't count for the long jump either!

No ladies, please!

Competitors who took part in the ancient Games, were easy to spot. They were all:

1. true Greeks
2. not slaves
3. covered in oil
4. stark naked

And, last but not least,

5. men

Women could compete in the Games in only one way, as the owner of a chariot and horses. Even then, women weren't allowed in as spectators. The law was that "any woman discovered at the Olympic Games should be thrown headlong from the mountain of Typaeum" (typped over the edge, in other words!).

Rule number four, of course, made it pretty tricky for a woman to sneak in without being noticed. That's why the rule was introduced, in fact. Because at one Games a woman named Kallipateira *did* sneak in...

ELIS SECRET SERVICE GAMES UNDERCOVER ENTRY SURVEILLANCE SECTION (G.U.E.S.S.)

REPORT AUTHOR: AGENT SPYONOUS

REPORT:

WHILST COVERING THE GAMES AT OLYMPIA UNDERCOVER I UNCOVERED SOMETHING NOT COVERED BY THE RULES.

ON THE DAY OF THE CHARIOT-RACING I SAW A SUSPICIOUS-LOOKING PERSON WEARING A LOOSE-FITTING GARMENT. I ASKED HIM WHO HE WAS.

'MY SON'S TRAINER', SAID THE PERSON.

THINKING THERE MIGHT BE SOMETHING GOING ON, I WAITED UNTIL THE RACE TOOK PLACE. AS THE PERSON'S SON WON HIS EVENT, THE PERSON MADE THE MISTAKE OF LEAPING OVER THE FENCE AND RUNNING ACROSS TO GIVE HIM A BIG KISS. WHAT A PLONKER!

ALL WAS THEN REVEALED! THE PERSON WAS NONE OTHER THAN KALLIPATEIRA, THE MOTHER OF THE CHAMPION **AND** A WOMAN.

ACTION: NONE TAKEN. THE JUDGES DECREED THAT KALLIPATEIRA BE FORGIVEN ON THIS OCCASION BECAUSE HER FAMILY ARE ALL GREAT ATHLETES AND PREVIOUS CHAMPIONS.

RECOMMENDATION: IN FUTURE, TRAINERS SHOULD NOT BE ALLOWED TO WEAR ANY LOOSE-FITTING GARMENTS. THEY SHOULDN'T BE ALLOWED TO WEAR ANY GARMENTS AT ALL.

GOOD IDEA. THAT WAY WE WON'T NEED ANY UNDERCOVER AGENTS. YOU'RE _FIRED_, SPYONOUS!

The modern Olympic Games

The ancient Games were finally abolished in AD 391 by the Emperor Theodosius. He was a Christian and objected to the Games because they honoured Zeus, a pagan god.

The Games had been going downhill for a while, though. Bribery and cheating had got worse and worse as athletes (and their kings) tried to capture the glory of being an Olympic champion.

By the time of Theodosius the reputation of the Olympic Games as a festival of honesty and fair play was pretty much gone.

But their memory lingered on. And, as memories do, they got rosier and rosier. People forgot all the grotty bits and thought only about how the athletes trained and struggled to get better at their sports for nothing more than the chance to win an olive wreath to stick on their heads.

Gradually, other 'Olympic' Games started up, trying to copy what had gone on all those years before in Greece. Well, not copy exactly...

Country games

One of these Games took place (and still does) in the small village of Wenlock in Shropshire. The Wenlock Olympian Games were started in 1850 by a man named William Penny Brookes. He was a doctor, and wanted to encourage outdoor sports because he thought it was more healthy for the villagers than sitting in a pub all day.

The Wenlock Games had some events that the ancient Greeks would have found very peculiar.

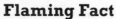

EYE WAS PROUD TO BE THERE

Flaming Fact

Although you didn't see quoits or cricket or a tea race, and nobody ran blindfolded, 'Wenlock' was still very much part of the London 2012 Olympics. One of the mascots was given that name in honour of the part that the Wenlock Games played in the revival of the Olympics. The other mascot was named 'Mandeville', after the hospital which was the birthplace of the Paralympics.

William Brookes wanted to get the Olympic Games started up again as more than just a small affair. He wanted to see an Olympics in which athletes of different countries competed against each other. His problem was that he couldn't get the support of England's important Amateur Athletic Club. They were an incredibly snooty bunch and most of their athletes came from the upper classes. They didn't like the idea of competing against grubby working-class people at all!

WORKING-CLASS OIK

UPPER-CLASS TWIT

But if Brookes didn't manage to convince the Amateur Athletic Club, he did convince one very important man: Baron Pierre de Coubertin, a French aristocrat. De Coubertin believed that playing sport made you a better person. He also thought it was great for bringing people of different countries together – certainly better than the usual way, of fighting a war. When he visited the Wenlock Games, and heard Brookes' idea of reviving the ancient Olympics, he decided to do something about it himself.

The difference between de Coubertin and Brookes was that the Frenchman knew a lot of important people (aristocrats tend to). In fact he knew so many important people that by 1894, only two years after visiting the Wenlock Games, de Coubertin had managed to set up an International Olympic Committee (IOC for short).

From there, things moved quickly. This committee met, made arrangements, and generally sorted things out. (Most unusual for a committee!) So much so that, just two years later, on Easter Monday 1896, the first 'Olympiad of the Modern Era' began. For obvious reasons it was staged in Athens, Greece.

Over the years, the Games grew in size with more and more countries taking part. More and more sports were introduced, too, including 'winter' sports like ice hockey …

… and figure skating.

In 1924 the summer and winter sports were separated, with the first Winter Olympics being held in Chamonix, France. (The 23rd Olympic Winter Games will be held in PyeongChang, South Korea, in 2018. Find out all about them in 'The Frozen Olympics' section on page 301.)

And so Pierre de Coubertin's dream has been realized … or has it? His dream was for the Olympics to be about athletes of all countries meeting in friendly, honest competition – no skulduggery or dirty tricks. Has that been the way? You'll soon find out.

So, start packing! Shorts, running shoes, swimming costume, tennis racket, hockey stick, weightlifting gear, spare horse … you'll need it all. Oh, yes – and you'd better pack the next chapter in too. It's your crucial guide to what's on…

FLAMING OLYMPIC EVENTS –
A DUFFER'S GUIDE

Are you a complete duffer when it comes to sports? Can you tell the difference between a hockey stick and a walking stick? Do you think that badminton is dreadful goodminton, or that weightlifting is carrying your bag home from school? Then this is the guide for you! Here's the idea behind every Olympic sport, with no confusing complications or jellylegging jargon to put you off.

Amazing athletics

You do one of three things in athletics: run, jump or throw something.

For a **running** race you go as fast as you can. If it's a short race you go faster, and if it's a long race you go slower. You can still win a short race if you go slower, of course, so long as you go faster than everybody else. In the same way, you can lose a long race by going slower than somebody else who's going slow faster. Get it?

Jumping is either long, high or very high. In long jumping you end up in a sand pit you're not allowed to play in. High jumping is more fun because you dive onto a bouncy castle (without the castle bit), but less fun because there's always a bar in the way! For very high jumping (called pole-vaulting) you get a better bounce, but you have to use a pole which is very awkward to fit into your bag.

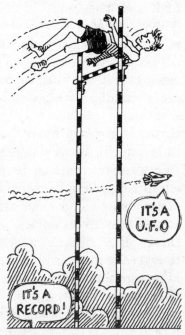

To remember the **throwing** events, think of school dinners. The idea is to throw something as far as you can, and you can choose between a discus (a sort of dinner-less dinner plate), a javelin (a fork with only one prong), a shot (a school-dinner dumpling, but not quite so hard or heavy) or a hammer (a school-dinner dumpling before it's let out of its saucepan).

People who can't make up their mind what they like best can go in for all of them. The **heptathlon** is for women and involves seven events: 100m hurdles, high and long jumps, shot put, javelin, 200 m and 800 m. Men are even worse at making up their minds, so they have a **decathlon** of ten events. They only sprint 100m instead of 200m – but have to do an extra 10m in the hurdles, run both 400m and 1500m races and discus-throw and pole-vault! Phew!

Jumping gymnastics

There are three gymnastic disciplines. In **artistic gymnastics** competitors score points using equipment like a horse you can't ride, a beam that doesn't shine and rings that don't make a sound. **Rhythmic gymnastics** involves exercises using things like ribbons which the competitors hope they'll turn into winning bows. Finally, to be the best at **trampoline gymnastics** you need plenty of spring in the summer! You have to be very supple for gymnastics, which is why some people call it gymelastics.

Curious combat

There are five combat sports.

Fencing is for people with a duel personality. You have a sword which isn't called a sword but either a foil, a sabre or an épée. Each of these has a handle end and a pointy end. The pointy end has a button on it so that it isn't too pointy. The idea is to touch the other person with the pointy end before they touch you. Get the point?

Boxing is like fencing without swords. In boxing you hit the other person with your fists. Boxers come in different weights. The lightest weight is 48 kg. This is called light flyweight, even though no 48 kg fly has ever been seen. The heaviest weight is superheavyweight, for supersized fighters of over 91 kg. Boxers have always been confused by maths,

which is why they fight for three rounds in a square ring and their referee never counts higher than ten!

The aim of **wrestling** is to get your opponent to lie down. Mothers are very good at this, especially when fighting children at bedtime, so its strange that women weren't allowed to compete in this event until 2004. Even so, they can still only take part in 'freestyle' wrestling, in which you can grab with your arms and legs. They're still banned from the second sort, known as 'Greco-Roman' wrestling, in which you can only use your arms. Perhaps the organizers are protecting the ladies because they think this is a more 'armful' event!

THIS WILL BE A SHORT FLING!

Judo is a throwing event (see Athletics), the differences being: **a)** you throw the other person; and **b)** it's not how far you throw them that matters,

33

but how often.

Finally, **tae kwon do** is a mixture of boxing and football because fighters can punch and kick each other. 'Tae kwon do' means 'the way of hands and feet' – but the idea is to get out of the way!

Terrific targets

There are two target sports, **archery** and **shooting**. In both the aim is to aim. It's also to hit as many bull's eyes as possible. In archery you use a bow and arrow. In shooting you use a gun and bullet to bull-hit. If the gun is a pistol or a rifle, shots which go in the air score no points at all. But if it's a shotgun then you aim in the air because you're trying to hit a clay 'pigeon' target.

Courting couples

These are sports played on a court – which is why they usually have a judge nearby. The idea with all of them is to score points by hitting something over a net and out of the reach of your opponent.

In **badminton**, what you hit is a shuttlecock. This is made out of feathers – which is why it flies so well!

Tennis players use a tennis ball. This is made out of rubber and makes a racket when you hit it. Scoring in tennis is very friendly. If you haven't scored any points at all, the judge calls you "love".

A small, light ball is used in **table-tennis**. This sport is played on a table, which is why serving properly is very important. Strangely, a perfect serve is one which the other player can't reach. If you manage this, everybody thinks you're ace.

It's in the net!

There are a number of team sports involving nets. Don't let them get you all tangled up!

In **football** you hit the ball into the net with your head or your foot; hand-ball is bad.

In **handball** foot-ball is bad; You hit the ball into the net with your hand.

In indoor **volleyball** you don't hit the ball into the net: that's bad. You use your hand to hit the ball *over* the net. The same goes for **beach volleyball** (in which you *don't* use a beachball).

In **basketball** you don't put the ball over the net: that's bad. You don't hit it into the net either: that's bad too. You *throw* the ball into the net.

Hockey is different from all of the others. Foot-ball is bad. Hand-ball is bad. Heading is very very bad. You hit the ball into the net using a wooden thing with a curved end. And if you're not very good at first, what you have to do is stick at it until you get better.

Oddball events

Two new ball sports are being introduced in 2016.

Golf is played by people who club together to try and knock a small ball into a not-quite-as-small hole. Golfers make lots of money, which is why golf is known as the mint with a hole in it.

Rugby Sevens involves a lot of wrestling and hand-ball playing – with a ball that isn't round and a goal that has no net! The aim is to try and score tries.

Antics in aquatics

Swimming is the cleanest of all sports, but the only one you can't learn from the bottom. The idea of all the swimming races is to get out of the water as quickly as possible. Events take place over different distances, and with the swimmers using different 'strokes'. Funnily enough, the fastest stroke is the crawl.

Synchronized swimming is rhythmic gymnastics for floating teams. Team members must do exactly the same as each other or their chances of winning go down the plughole.

Diving is dead simple. Watch carefully, and you'll see there are only three parts to it:

1. go up to a high place;

2. jump off and pretend you're doing gymnastics instead; and

3. land in the water.

Divers don't have to be swimmers, but it helps. They have to do three dives, and drowning after the first won't score very well. Oh, yes – the diver that makes the biggest splash with the judges is usually the one who makes the smallest splash. The same goes for **synchronized diving**, in which two divers try to look the same as each other. If they don't, their medal chances take a nosedive.

Water polo can only be played at fun times, because you need to have a ball in the pool with you. There are two aims of the game: **1** to throw the ball into the other team's goal; and **2** not to drown. Think of water polo as being a bit like handball with a lot of drips.

Weird water events

There are three outdoor water events, in which the last thing you want to do is go in the water.

Competitors use different equipment to stop this happening.

Rowing has rowing boats long enough for all team members to sit down in a row, and the idea is to see who can go backwards the fastest.

Canoeing and **Kayaking** both allow competitors to paddle without getting wet; kayakers are more comfortable because they can sit down, whereas canoers have to do it on their knees.

Sailing can be difficult to join because it requires an expensive yacht. The cheaper option is to go for a surfboard, which is a yacht with no sides and just a tiny bottom.

Rip-roaring riding

There are two riding sports in the Olympics and they're both very similar. The first is **cycling**, in which cycles are ridden in an arena, on roads or across country. The second sport is called **equestrianism**, in which you ride ... yes, an *equus*. It's the Latin word for horse.

Cycles and horses can be tricky to tell apart:

- they both have saddles
- neither needs petrol
- both leave marks to show where they've been
- both have riders wearing coloured outfits and hard hats.

Top tip: to tell the difference, wait until they stop moving. Horses don't fall over.

Murderous multiples

Last, but not least, for totally hyperactive athletes there are two ultimate events:

Modern pentathlon involves:

- **riding** a horse, until it says "neigh, no more!"…
- **fencing** your way out of trouble in a sword duel…
- **shooting** your way out of even more trouble with a pistol…
- **swimming** your way to freedom across a river, before finally…
- **running** 4,000 m to complete your mission!

The absolute murder pentathlon might be a better description!

Triathlon: At least competitors in the modern pentathlon get to rest between events. Not so for tortured triathletes. They have to swim 1.5 km, jump straight on a bike (without getting dried) and pedal 40 km, then leap off and run 10 km to the finish. Gulp. It's a wonder the sport wasn't called the cry-athlon instead!

OK, that's it! Now you've had a full run-down of the running events, a crash course in the combat events, a deadly accurate guide to the target events and you're one jump ahead about the gymnastics.

So, let's go! First stop the opening ceremony. The fun and Games are about to begin!

STRIKE A LIGHT! –
THE OPENING CEREMONY

Here we are then. So, what's going to happen?

Well, the ancient Games had an opening ceremony. Remember – when the athletes and judges did a lot of swearing? (Before the events got under way and they did a lot more swearing!)

It's the same with the modern Olympics. In 1896, though, the ceremony was over and done with pretty quickly. There was a procession of all the competitors, the Games were declared open, a bugle sounded and that was it – the first event began.

Nowadays, though, it's not so simple. Over the years more and more bits have been added to the opening ceremony. Let's join the Olympic 2016 parade in Rio de Janeiro, Brazil.

The procession (first happened in 1896)

First into the stadium is the Olympic flag. Then come the different national teams. Hang on, it's not us yet! Greece always come first, because that's where the Olympics began. After them come the teams of the other countries, in alphabetical order. The host country comes last (probably to make sure the crowd stays awake until the end of the procession!).

Olympic oddity

In 1988 the Olympic games were held in Seoul, South Korea. Greece led in, as usual – but instead of Afghanistan there followed Gabon and Ghana – and there was a good reason for it! What could it have been?

Answer: The Korean alphabet begins with G, not A.

Boring speeches (1896)

Here we are at last! That procession took well over an hour! So, what's the last thing you want to have now? A boring speech? Sorry, that's just what you're going to get. Yawn…

Aha! Good news. The VIP is on his/her feet. The VIP's job is to declare the Games open, and his/her speech will be dead short. How can we be sure? It's already written!

41

The Olympic oath (1920)

Right, the VIP's sitting down again. Now what? Well, remember in the ancient Games the competitors swore an oath not to cheat or get up to any funny business? That's the next bit. Up you go, you can do it. On behalf of all the athletes you say:

IN THE NAME OF ALL THE COMPETITORS I PROMISE THAT WE SHALL TAKE PART IN THESE OLYMPIC GAMES, RESPECTING AND ABIDING BY THE RULES WHICH GOVERN THEM, COMMITTING OURSELVES TO A SPORT WITHOUT DOPING AND WITHOUT DRUGS, IN THE TRUE SPIRIT OF SPORTSMANSHIP, FOR THE GLORY OF SPORT AND THE HONOUR OF OUR TEAMS.

In other words, "we all promise to play fair". (But it doesn't always happen – as you'll find out in the Champion Cheats chapter!)

The Olympic flag (1920)

Not going up the pole yet, are you? Good. Because that's the job of the Olympic flag. There it goes. It's white, with five interlocking rings coloured blue, black, red, yellow and green (because, in 1920, at least one of these colours appeared in the flag of each country taking part in the Games). It's supposed to represent five continents of the world being united in sport.

The Olympic motto (1924)

The motto contains just three words: *Citius, Altius, Fortius.*

The only problem with it as a motto is that they're Latin words and most people don't know what they mean. (You too, eh? How about your teacher? Oh, dear.)

So, here they are in English: *Swifter, Higher, Stronger.*

Whatever their particular sport, every single Olympic competitor is trying to perform to the very best of their ability.

The Olympic flame (1928)

OK, the ceremony's hotting up a bit now. We're getting ready to light the Olympic flame. It'll stay alight all the while the Games are on. Now, where's that flaming torch...

The torch relay (1936)

Ah, here it comes. It's being carried by the last runner in a relay that's brought it all the way from Olympia. (Or runners. At London 2012 the flame was divided between seven young athletes). The idea comes from a fun event in the Ancient Games called a lampadedromia – a lamp race. It was a relay race except that, instead of a baton, the runners carried a lighted torch! The winners were the first team home with the torch still alight, and to them went the honour of lighting the sacred flame.

Fancy organizing the relay another year? Right, here's what you'll have to do:

① GO TO OLYMPIA. (THE ONE IN GREECE, NOT WEST LONDON.)

② FIND A GREEK LADY.

③ ASK HER TO DRESS UP IN ANCIENT ROBES!

THE TORCH RELAY

④ GIVE HER A TORCH TO HOLD.

⑩ REPEAT STEP ⑧.... UNTIL **THE OLYMPIC STADIUM IS REACHED!**

⑨ AFTER A WHILE GIVE THE TORCH TO SOMEBODY ELSE.

⑤ MAKE SURE IT'S A SUNNY DAY. IF NOT COME BACK TOMORROW.

⑧ START RUNNING TOWARDS THE COUNTRY WHERE THE OLYMPIC GAMES ARE TO BE HELD.

⑦ SAY THANK YOU NICELY AND TAKE THE TORCH.

⑥ GET THE GREEK LADY TO LIGHT THE TORCH USING ONLY THE RAYS OF THE SUN (NO BATTERIES! IT'S NOT THAT SORT OF TORCH!)

MOST IMPORTANT: DO NOT LET THE TORCH GO OUT! EVEN MORE IMPORTANT: IF IT DOES GO OUT AND YOU HAVE TO LIGHT IT AGAIN, MAKE SURE NOBODY SEES YOU!

The first relay in 1936 covered 3,000 km, with the torch being carried by runners doing 1 km each. This is still the way it's done, although sometimes part of the journey is made by sea or air.

(Or laser beam! For the Montreal Olympics in 1976 the flame's energy was used to send a laser beam from Greece which ended up by lighting an identical torch in Canada.)

At the end of the relay the final runner entered the stadium and trotted round the track (trying not to sneeze!), climbed a flight of steps and transferred the Olympic flame to a large cauldron shaped like a cereal bowl. The bowl of flames snapped, crackled and popped the whole time the Games were on. That still happens … only differently.

In Barcelona in 1992 they tried something different. The runner used the Olympic torch to light an archer's arrow … slowly, the archer took aim at the big bowl, high up on the far side of the stadium … he drew back the bowstring … fired … the flaming arrow shot off into the night sky … and the Olympic flame burst into life!

It looked like the archer had been incredibly accurate, but in fact he could have missed by a mile. Things had been rigged so that the flame would light up anyway.

At Sydney in 2000 the flame was to be lit by Australia's 400 m gold-medal hope, Cathy Freeman. Perhaps to save her energy for the real athletics, the organizers decided not to make her run up steps to the cauldron. It would come down to her. All went well until the cauldron, now burning merrily, was meant to go back up again. The track it was running on got stuck for a couple of minutes.

Flaming Fact

The London 2012 cauldron was gas-powered, but turned right down when the stadium was empty. One even 'greener' proposal, though, was for it to burn scraps of wood instead!

Phew! That's the opening ceremony over. All very nice, but now it's time to get on with the real stuff. Three weeks of running and jumping and swimming and cycling and generally going round the bend.

So, better have a quick look round while you've got a chance. Where's everything happening? And who are you going to be up against...

HOT HOLIDAYS AND COLD WARS – THE COMPETITORS

It took the host city a whole year to prepare for the ancient Games. Sorting out the stadium and getting ready for the crowds of competitors, judges and spectators was a major task. (Pity they didn't have a Heracles around to help!)

Nowadays, though, even a year wouldn't be anything like long enough.

The host city is chosen *seven* years in advance! Rio de Janeiro, the host of the 2016 Games, was chosen on 2nd October 2009.

Why so long? Because there's usually a lot of building to do and a lot of arrangements to make. Every sport in the Games needs its own stadium or playing area, for a start. Then there are the people who will be coming, from 201 different countries.

The numbers game

Try these numbers questions about the 2016 Games...

1. About how many competitors are expected?

2. How many countries will be represented?

3. How many volunteers are being recruited to turn up and help the Games run smoothly?

a) 450 b) 4,500 c) 45,000

4. How many people are expected to watch the Games on television?

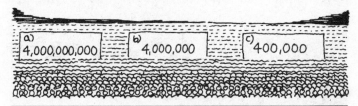

a) 4,000,000,000 b) 4,000,000 c) 400,000

Add to all these the hundreds of newspaper reporters ... the TV and film crews ... the hot-dog sellers ... and it all adds up to a lot of people needing somewhere to stay and something to eat.

The athletes come first, of course. A special 'village' is built for them to live in. Although sometimes 'village' is too grand a word...

Six things you didn't know about Olympic villages

1. In the ancient Games they didn't have one! The athletes had to find somewhere to live themselves. Even worse, all those sweaty runners, wrestlers, boxers, pankrationists and charioteers had to share just two bath houses! It's a wonder they weren't called the Oh-stinky Games.

2. The 1920 Games were held in Antwerp, in Belgium. The 'village' was actually a school building.

3. Los Angeles in 1932 saw the first purpose-built village – for men only! To make sure that women athletes (women of any description, in fact) didn't get in, the village was guarded by cowboys. The women athletes – all 127 of them – shared a hotel.

4. In 1952, two Olympic villages were built. One for the men and one for the women, you think? No – one for the communist countries (who were suspicious of everybody else) and one for everybody else.
5. For the 1980 Winter Olympics at Lake Placid, USA, brand new accommodation was built to house competitors and officials. Even so, when the Games ended, everybody left very quickly. The place was being turned into a prison!

6. The Olympic village, like all the sites for Sydney in 2000, was designed to be as 'green' as possible. Rather than use good drinking water for loo-flushing, for example, recycled water (like rainwater) was used instead. Just as well: during the course of the Games the athletes got through no fewer than 370,000 toilet rolls – that's enough paper to stretch 15,000 kms!

Countries taking part

More and more competitors and countries have joined the Olympics since they were started again in 1896. Then there were just 311 competitors – and 230 of those were from Greece, where the Games were taking place!

In fact, for the first few Olympiads, most of the athletes did come from the host country. Why? Because of the time taken to travel from overseas. In those days, the fastest way of travelling was by boat. And there were other problems – as the team from America found out...

MRS IDA HO,
IDAHO,
U.S.A.

Athens, Greece

15TH April, 1896

Dear Mom,

Are we having an amazing time! I've sure got a lot of news to report from here in little ol' Greece. Some of it's been bad and some of it's been good- so here goes, BAD NEWS: The boat trip from America took 17 days. Not what you'd call plain sailing!

GOOD NEWS: When we finally got here, though, the Greek people were real pleased to see us. They threw a party for us and kept us up all night eating and drinking. Especially drinking.

BAD NEWS: Next morning we found out that we'd got our dates wrong. The Greeks run a different calendar to us and the start of the Games wasn't a week away like we thought. They were due to start that day! And for some reason I had a real bad headache, Mommie...

GOOD NEWS: Even so, we won 11 gold medals between us. Maybe we should go drinking every night! (Only joking, Mom! I stuck to milk shakes all the time.)

Your loving son and Olympic athlete,
Hank

53

Over the years, travel has become a bit easier! With the Olympic Games growing in popularity, more and more countries have sent teams to compete. In Rio in 2016 no fewer than 205 countries are expected to be represented.

Guns or Games

Baron de Coubertin's idea that the Games should take the place of wars hasn't always managed to get through to the Generals, though. In ancient times, wars would be held up while the Olympics were on. Every king would sign a 'peace treaty' saying something like:

I, KING OF WHATSIT, DO HEREBY AGREE THAT FOR THE DURATION OF THE SACRED OLYMPIAD, WE WHATSITS WILL NOT TAKE UP ARMS, PURSUE LEGAL DISPUTES, OR ANYTHING ELSE LIKELY TO ENDANGER ATHLETES AND SPECTATORS HEADING FOR OLYMPIA. AND IF WE BREAK THIS AGREEMENT, THEN WE WHATSITS WILL PAY A FINE OF ONE TALENT OF SILVER TO ZEUS AT OLYMPIA.

In modern times it hasn't worked this way. The Games have been cancelled instead. This has happened three times.

- In 1916, the 6th Olympiad was given the bullet because World War I got in the way.
- In 1940 and 1944, the 12th and 13th Olympiads were bombed out because World War II was being fought.

Did you know?

Olympiad numbers count, even if the Games don't take place. So the Games in Rio de Janeiro will be called the 31st Olympiad, even though they'll only be the 28th Games to have been held.

I'm not playing with you, so there!

Even though the Olympics have been held at all other times, not everybody has been there! In fact only Australia, France, Greece, Great Britain and Switzerland have been at every Games since 1896. How come? Well, athletes swear an oath that sport will come first – but the politicians don't. And what a mess that makes…

- In 1920 Germany, Austria, Hungary and Turkey (the countries on the losing side in World War I) weren't invited.
- By 1924 Germany still hadn't been forgiven; they weren't invited back until the next Games in 1928.
- In 1948, Germany and Japan (the countries on the losing side in World War II) weren't invited. Russia and the other communist countries were invited but decided to stay away.
- From 1964 to 1992 South Africa weren't invited because of their policy of apartheid (treating people differently depending on the colour of their skin).

- In 1980 the Olympics were held in Russia. As they'd just invaded Afghanistan, the United States, West Germany and Japan stayed away as a protest.
- In 1984, the Games were held in the United States – so Russia stayed at home to pay America back for 1980!

Money, money, money

For many years (until 1992) the other restriction was that you weren't allowed in to the Olympics if you were a professional – that is, if you earned money from playing sport. Baron de Coubertin insisted on this. His view was that a professional's only aim is to win the prize money and that they couldn't care tuppence for simply taking part (but if they had cared tuppence that would have made them professionals, wouldn't it? Hmm...).

For a long time, the Baron's successors said the same, although nobody really believed that every athlete taking part didn't really earn money from their sports. But, so long as they weren't found out, it was all right...

The greatest athlete in the world

Jim Thorpe of America won both the pentathlon and decathlon in the 1912 Games (a total of 15 events!) by wide margins. When presenting him with his medals, King Gustav V of Sweden told Thorpe, "Sir, you are the greatest athlete in the world!"

But a year later it was revealed that Thorpe had once accepted a small amount of money for playing baseball in his youth – which, according to the the the Olympics organizers, made him a professional. Even though the people he beat in the 1912 Games refused to accept his medals, Thorpe still had them taken away and his name was removed from the Olympic records.

It wasn't until 1982 – 70 years later, and 30 years after Thorpe's death in 1953 – that this unfair decision was reversed and his medals given back to his family.

'Ere we go ... competitors & teams

Until 1912, there were no official teams. Competitors entered as individuals, or as groups of friends who fancied the outing – anybody who turned up could enter! Like the Irishman, John Boland, who in 1896 just happened to be on holiday in Greece...

In 1896 John Boland won the tennis singles! He also teamed up with a German partner and won the doubles. An ace performer!

Another winner was an Australian, Edwin Flack, who'd been working in London when he heard about the Olympics. He promptly took a month's holiday and toddled off to Greece to take part. When he came back he had something really different to show around the office – winning medals for the 800 and 1,500 metres races.

Some countries did send teams to Greece, but they weren't official. The Americans, for instance, were all college students and had arranged to go together.

As for the British team – well, most of the best athletes didn't go. Why? Because the best were all incredibly snooty Oxford and Cambridge University students – and they were objecting because the invitation to take part in the Games had been written in French!

I SAY! THAT'S NOT BRITISH!

AND IT'S NOT CRICKET!

Trials and tribulations!

Nowadays, countries send official teams, and most of them hold trials to choose the people who will go to the Olympics.

One US runner had a particularly tough time winning his place. Boyd Gittens was taking part in the trial for the 100 metre hurdles race in the 1972 Olympics in Mexico. This is what happened...

1. He got to his marks.

2. He got set.

3. When the starter's gun went off, he flew down the track.

4. The trouble was, a pigeon flew down the track too. And, unlike Boyd, the pigeon hadn't been to the toilet before the race. So...

5. The pigeon let rip there and then. And, as we all know, droppings drop...

6. Which this one did – right in Boyd Gitten's eye...

7. Knocking out his contact lens! He couldn't go on and – you've guessed it – he had to 'drop' out of the race!

There was almost a happy ending, though. They ran the trial again. This time, Boyd qualified for the team and went to Mexico – where this happened...

1. He didn't get to his marks.

2. He didn't get set.

He'd got an injured leg and couldn't run!

Oly the slowly

Not all teams are picked in the same way, though. In 1976, Olemus Charles from Haiti ran the worst-ever time for the 10 km race. He took over 42 minutes (the usual time is about 28 mins) and by the time he finished, everybody else was getting changed. It was then discovered that Olemus wasn't really a runner at all, and he'd never competed in a big event. Haiti hadn't held any trials at all. The dictator of the country had given out places in the

Olympics as rewards. Oly the Slowly had won his trip through being a good office worker!

Eric the Eel and Paula the Porpoise

Eric Moussambani and Paula Barila Bolopa arrived at the Sydney 2000 Games as a completely unknown two-person swimming team from Equatorial Guinea – but they went back famous!

Was this because of their record-breaking performances in the pool? Well, yes ... and no. Eric and Paula's performances were record-breaking in a way. They were just about the worst the Olympics had ever seen!

Eric set the standard in his 100 m freestyle race. After the other two swimmers in his heat dropped out, Eric had to swim alone. In he dived – to show everybody how a front crawl could be exactly that: he swam on his front ... and crawled. Roared on by the crowd, Eric finally struggled home in 1 minute 52 seconds, just about a minute slower than all the other heat winners. "I thought I had a good chance over the last 50 metres," said Eric, "– of drowning!"

A couple of days later, wearing borrowed goggles and swimming cap, it was Paula's turn. In her 50 m freestyle heat, she splashed home in 1.03.97, taking well over twice as long as the heat winner's 26.8 seconds. "It was further than I thought," said Paula.

61

Afterwards it was revealed that the biggest swimming pools in Equatorial Guinea are 20 m long and if you want to train for a 50 m length you have to do it in a river.

They'd only got to the Olympics as part of a scheme to give athletes from smaller countries a chance to compete. Quickly nicknamed Eric the Eel and Paula the Porpoise the two 'swimmers' became overnight celebrities, not least because they reminded everybody of the words that have been displayed during every opening ceremony since 1932:

"The most important thing is not to win but to take part, just as the most important thing in life is not the triumph but the struggle. The essential thing is not to have conquered but to have fought well."

Ladies AND gentlemen!

As we saw earlier, women weren't allowed to enter the ancient Games. Well, when Baron de Coubertin started the modern Olympics his view was that exactly the same number should enter the modern Olympics! He said:

He got his way in 1896 – not a single woman was allowed to take part! In 1900 things improved slightly (they could hardly get any worse) with 12 women taking part. Only two events were open to them: tennis and golf!

Over the years, though, more and more women have taken part in the Games. In 2012 over 4,000 women competed.

What's more, women now compete in every Summer Olympics sport. In fact the position has now been reversed. Which of these 2016 sports won't have male competitors?

1. Archery
2. Beach Volleyball
3. Cycling
4. Equestrian
5. Hockey

6. Judo
7. Sailing
8. Rhythmic Gymnastics
9. Synchronized Swimming
10. Taekwondo

How rude!

It's been a long struggle for acceptance, though. Lots of nasty things have been said, and women have had to prove people wrong. Here are some of the times it's happened!

● In 1928, women competed in athletics events for the first time: the 100 m, 800 m, 4 x 100 m relay, discus and high jump. After the 800 m, Baron de Coubertin complained that the tired women provided "a very unedifying spectacle for the spectators". After this, women weren't allowed to run more than 200 m until 1960. They now have their own marathon race and football tournament.

● A woman is the only athlete to have won medals at running, jumping and throwing events. In 1932, Mildred 'Babe' Didrikson (USA) won the 80 m hurdles and javelin gold medals, and got silver in the high jump.

64

• When the 31-year-old Dutch woman athlete Francina 'Fanny' Blankers-Koen turned up at the London Olympics in 1948, the British team manager, Jack Crump, said she was "too old to win anything". She promptly won four gold medals in the 100 m, 200 m, 80 m hurdles and 4 x 100 m relay – and Jack crumpled!

But of all the brilliant women athletes there have been at the Olympics, perhaps the two most unlikely were these...

The two sickly kids

Dawn Fraser was born on 4 September 1937. She was the youngest of eight children, four boys and four girls, living in an old semi-detached house.

The house was in a run-down area, not far from where the ships lay at anchor in Sydney docks. It was as if Dawn Fraser was meant to be close to water.

She was spoilt pretty rotten as a baby. All those brothers and sisters to cuddle her! "Dawnie, Dawnie," they'd sing into her ear, and she'd gurgle merrily.

It wasn't long, though, before the gurgling turned to coughing. As she grew up it seemed that if there was a cold going, Dawn would catch it. The trouble was, it wouldn't just give her a runny nose, then go away. It would hang around, spreading to her lungs and ending up in a bout of asthma. When this happened it was scary for everybody.

"I can't breathe!" she'd gasp. "It feels like I've got a kangaroo sitting on my chest!" (This might sound funny, but it wasn't. Kangaroos are as heavy as a small car.) Sometimes the asthma was so bad Dawn would have to sleep sitting up in bed, afraid to lay down in case it made her start coughing again.

And then, one day in 1943, when Dawn was six years old, her brother Don took her to the swimming pool. As she splashed around in the water, breathing in the warm, moist air, Dawn felt something happening to her. Her lungs felt better. She didn't feel like coughing so much.

Maybe if she learnt to swim it would help her even more...

Thousands of miles away, in the Southern state of Tennessee in the United States of America, another little girl was having troubles with her health. Her name was Wilma Rudolph. She was three years younger than Dawn Fraser, but also from a big family. Dawn might have thought her family of eight was big, but if she'd had the chance Wilma would have told Dawn she didn't know what 'big' meant –

Wilma was the youngest of 12 children!

Wilma's family suffered by being picked on because they were black. They were also very poor, and often hungry. Like Dawn Fraser though, the only thing Wilma didn't miss out on was illness. As the years went by, Wilma caught scarlet fever, double pneumonia (a disease in both lungs) and then, at the age of six, the worst of the lot – polio. It left her with a paralysed right leg.

"Good job there's a lot of us, Wilma," her brothers and sisters would say, "we can take it in turns to rub it back to life for you!"

And rub her leg they did, four times a day, every day. Wilma did her bit too. She was absolutely determined to walk like everybody else. But she had to be patient. She still needed a metal brace on her leg when she was eight, and couldn't walk far without having somebody to help her.

She kept working and exercising. It took her a further four years to make her leg strong enough to stand on her own. She was able to swap the leg brace for a special shoe – but still she wasn't satisfied. Now she wanted to run properly.

Her brothers played basketball. With so many of them, they almost had their own team! Wilma began to join in, hopping around in her special shoe. She played and played, exercised and exercised, until one day the shoe felt just too heavy. Wilma took it off. It was the day she'd dreamt of. In her bare feet, the 12-year-old Wilma Rudolph started running...

Dawn Fraser was 15 by then, and still swimming. After that first time in the public swimming pool, she'd gone as often as she could (usually getting in for free by jumping over the turnstile in the middle of a gang of boys). Her brother Don had taught her to swim, sometimes by diving from the high board with Dawn on his back!

She'd joined a swimming club, and won her first race – against grown women! By the time she was 12 she was winning races regularly, and looking forward to the day when she could pick up the small cash prizes her swimming club gave to winners who were over 16.

And then – she was banned! After winning a championship race, Dawn Fraser was accused of being a professional! The reason? Because of the money prizes the club gave. In spite of the fact that Dawn wasn't 16, hadn't won any money, and didn't even belong to the club any more, she wasn't allowed to enter competitions for 18 months. But she kept on training, riding her bike 20 miles a day to get to swimming lessons.

Dawn Fraser wanted an Olympic gold medal...

By then, so did Wilma Rudolph. Once she'd started running, she couldn't stop. Her legs, a pain for so long, were now her greatest joy. They were growing, long and graceful. Her speed was improving, day by day. She was getting faster, racing over 100 metres and 200 metres in quicker and quicker times.

By the age of 15, the painful days of limping and being helped around were far behind her. She was now winning American sprint championships. Asked about this miracle, Wilma would just joke about the size of her family. "I had to learn to run fast," she'd say, "otherwise there was nothing left to eat by the time I got to the table!"

Just one year later, Wilma Rudolph found herself sitting on an aeroplane. The girl who couldn't walk properly only a few years before was on her way to compete in the 1956 Olympic Games – in Melbourne, Australia, the home of Dawn Fraser. Dawn was competing, too.

The two sickly girls had made it to the top of the class.

That year, Dawn Fraser won the 100 m freestyle swimming gold medal in a world-record time. Four years later, in 1960, Dawn won the 100 m freestyle again, the first woman to win this race two Games in succession. As if that wasn't enough, she won it again in 1964

In 1956, at just 16 years of age, Wilma Rudolph won a bronze medal as a member of the American 4 x 100 m relay team. Her time was to come. In 1960, Wilma Rudolph was the talk of the Olympics as she won the 100 m and 200 m sprints and ran a stunning last leg to help her country to victory in the 4 x 100 m relay.

ABSOLUTE TORCH-URE - FLAMING OLYMPICS TRAINING

To be an Olympic champion needs dedication. That runner or swimmer or cyclist or boxer or gymnast has probably given up everything to train for their running, swimming, cycling, boxing or ... er, gymnasticalling.

So, do flaming Olympians enjoy training, or do they find it absolute torch-ure? Well, training to be a champion has always been tough...

How did competitors train for the ancient Games?

1. Competitors used to rub linseed oil into their skin. **True or False?**

2. Everybody started training ten months before the Games. **True or False?**

3. If you weren't fit enough the day before the Games started, you wouldn't be allowed to compete. **True or False?**

4. Boxers strengthened their muscles by breaking up the ground with a pick. **True or False?**

5. Discus and javelin throwers trained by listening to pop music. **True or False?**

6. Runners warmed up by beating their vests. **True or False?**

7. Shortly before the Games started, competitors went on a strict diet of bread and milk. **True or False?**

Answers:

1. **False.** Linseed oil is what you rub into a cricket bat! They used olive oil. This was to keep the dirt out and prevent sunburn.
2. **True.** They also had to swear an oath that they would train properly. No sick notes from Mum.
3. **False.** You had to be fit enough one month before.
4. **True.** Then, when they got to the Games they picked on each other!
5. **True.** Music was played along with these events to help the athletes get the rhythm they needed to throw well.
6. **False.** They beat their chests – they couldn't beat their vests because they ran in the nude. They also ran on the spot and did short, sharp sprints – just like runners do today.
7. **False.** They went on a strict diet of cheese and water.

Oy, Mister

British long jumper Jade Johnson wasn't sure how things worked when, aged thirteen, she turned up at a running track in Tooting, in London. So she simply asked the first official-looking person she saw, 'Can I join in please, mister?'

Fortunately he said yes. Within four months Jade had qualified for the final of a national indoor sprint competition. She finished second – and cried her eyes out. It was the first race she'd ever lost!

Jade then switched to the long jump, so successfully that she won Commonwealth and European silver medals in the event. She came seventh in the Beijing 2008 Olympics final. Jumping Jade managed all this in spite of suffering from a strange allergy: to what?

a) sand

b) suntan lotion

c) lycra

Answer: a) A bit tricky when you spend your time jumping into a bit full of the stuff! That's why Jade Johnson competes in a pair of knee-high socks.

Flaming food fads

As we're always being told, eating the right things makes you healthy. (And eating the *wrong* things makes you *happy*!) For an athlete, of course, eating the right sort of food is an important part of getting into peak condition. So, if you want to be a champ you've got to chomp the right stuff!

Here are some of the foods Olympic champions have eaten. Not all of them were terribly healthy – but they worked! Why not check out other people's trolleys the next time you're at a supermarket? You might spot an Olympian in training!

● **Dried figs**

They certainly made Charmis the Spartan run! He trained on dried figs before winning the two-stade foot race in 668 BC.

● **French wine**

The French runners in the 1932 Olympics in Los Angeles

73

claimed wine was an essential part of their diet. Although alcohol was banned in the USA at that time, their wine was allowed.

● **Chewing gum**

Eddie Tolan, 200 m and 100 m winner in 1932, liked to get stuck into his gum while he set about chewing up the other runners.

● **Chicken nuggets**

Usain Bolt (Jamaica) won the 100 m at Beijing in 2008 after a hearty meal of chicken nuggets. He was worried about getting an upset stomach and thought they'd be a safer bet than a Chinese take-away!

● **Raw carrots, raw onions, raw spinach, raw cabbage, raw most things**

Herb Elliott, the Australian 1,500 m champion in 1960, had a diet of natural foods which he always ate raw.

● **5 yoghurts, 10 pieces of fruit, 4 cups of tea, 2 coffees, 2 pastries, large amounts of meat, fish, milk and cheese – and as much parsley as possible**

This was what Mahmoud Gammoudi of Tunisia (who won the 5,000 m in 1968) used to eat – every day!

● **Sherry and raw eggs (but they must be mixed together!)**

The USA athletes Murchison, Scholz, Paddock and Kirksey (all 100 m finalists in 1920) used to drink this mixture. Ugh!

● **One ox (freshly-sacrificed)**
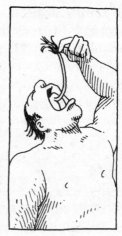
Milo of Croton was the strong-man superstar of the ancient Games, winning the wrestling title in six successive Olympiads. He was so strong that it's said he once lifted a four-year-old ox that had just been sacrificed and carried it round the stadium on his shoulders. What was the secret of his great strength? Well, he was no vegetarian. When he put the ox down he ate it – in a day!

● **Champagne**
Eleanor Holm (USA) was a swimmer who just loved clubbing. She'd won the 1932 gold for 100 m backstroke and was all set to do the same in 1936 as the USA team set sail for Berlin. It didn't happen. After being caught drinking on board, the strict American Olympic Committee expelled her from the team. Afterwards, Holm said: "I always have a glass or two of champagne after training!"

Add some zest to your training
There's no substitute for hard work, though. If you want to be an Olympic champion you've got to grit your teeth (or take them out) and get on with it. But it can be boring, so it's a good idea to do something just that little bit different now and again to liven things up. Which dodges livened up training for these four champion athletes?

1. Emil Zatopeck of Czechoslovakia won the 10,000 m in 1948. In 1952, he won the 5,000 m, 10,000 m and the marathon! How did he train?
a) He ran with a sack of potatoes on his back.
b) He ran with a lump of concrete on his back.
c) He ran with Mrs Zatopeck on his back.

2. Kelly Holmes of Great Britain won both the women's 800m and 1500m in 2004. But according to her mum, when she was younger, heroic Holmes sometimes needed encouragement to train. What provided this encouragement?
a) a very loud alarm clock
b) the family dog
c) cream doughnuts

3. Harold Abrahams of Great Britain won the 100 m in 1924. What did his coach, Sam Mussabini, make him do?
a) The splits.
b) Pick up pieces of paper.
c) Ballet dance.

4. Paavo Nurmi of Finland won the 10,000 m track and 10,000 m cross-country in 1920. Four years later he won the 10,000 m cross-country again, together with the 1,500 m and 5,000 m on the track. All told, he won nine Olympic medals. What did he do in training?
a) Race against mail trains.
b) Race against cars.
c) Race against ice skaters.

Answers:

1. c) – and Zatopeck's wife, Dana, was no shrimp, either. She won the women's javelin in the 1952 Olympics! In training Zatopeck would also get up at 6 am every day (leaving his wife in bed) and run 10–25 miles wearing his army boots. That way his legs felt stronger when he had his running spikes on.

2. b) According to Kelly's mum, the dog would drag her along and get her running. Maybe this explains her speed: the dog's name was 'Harley' – which is a make of a motorbike!

3. b) – but he had to do it with his running spikes! To help make sure Harold was stretching his legs far enough, the pieces of paper were placed exactly where Mussabini thought Abrahams' feet should land during a race.

4. a) Nurmi would also do short sprints when he finished work, go for a run in the forest before dinner and then end the day by jumping and throwing his arms about.

It ain't half hot mum!

Sometimes there's extra training that athletes have to go in for – it's called acclimatisation. If the Games are being held in a cold country, for instance, and you come from a hot one, then you need to do some training in cold temperatures to get used to what it's like. On the other hand, if the Games are being held in a city high above sea-level (where the air is thinner, making it harder to breathe), then you need to do some training at that height.

Pretend you're the 50 km walker, Don Thompson, in 1960. It's going to be hot and humid in Rome, and you come from chilly Britain. This is how to acclimatize.

It worked for Don Thompson. He won the gold medal.

The right gear

Wearing the right clothing can also be important. That was certainly so in one event at the ancient Games. This was the 'running-in-armour' race, in which every competitor had to dress head to toe in the armour of a Greek soldier.

Well – it was head to toe until the day this happened…

ORSIPPES TRIPS UP!!

THE 'RUNNING-IN-ARMOUR' RACE ENDED IN A SENSATION AT YESTERDAY'S OLYMPIC GAMES IN ELIS WHEN HOT FAVOURITE ORSIPPES OF MEGARA LOST HIS TITLE AND A LOT MORE BESIDES!

AT THE STARTING LINE, THOUGH THERE'D BEEN NO HINT OF WHAT WAS TO COME. ORSIPPES LOOKED SPLENDID IN HIS FULL OUTFIT. HIS HELMET SHONE. HIS CHEST PLATE SHONE. HIS LEG PLATES SHONE HIS SHORTS DIDN'T SHINE THEY SHIMMERED. AND AS FOR HIS SHIELD... NEVER HAS A SOLDIER'S SHIELD SHIMMERED AND SHONE LIKE THAT SOLDIER'S SHIELD.

THE STARTER CALLED THEM TO THEIR MARKS. SHIMMERING ORSIPPES SHWAGGERED FORWARD WITH A CONFIDENT SHMILE ON HIS FACE.

AS THE RACE STARTED ORSIPPES WENT QUICKLY INTO THE LEAD, HIS ARMOUR CLANKING LOUDLY. THE OTHER RUNNERS WERE OBVIOUSLY RATTLED. IT LOOKED AS THOUGH THE RACE WAS AS GOOD AS OVER.

SUDDENLY, ORSIPPE'S BELT CAME UNDONE! HIS SHORTS BEGAN TO SLIP. ANXIOUSLY, HE GAVE A LOOK BEHIND. IT WAS PRETTY CLEAR WHAT HAD HAPPENED.

SEEING THE OTHERS ON HIS TAIL ORSIPPES TRIED TO BELT A BIT FASTER. IT WAS NO GOOD. AS HE APPROACHED THE WINNING LINE EVERYBODY IN THE STADIUM COULD SEE THE END WAS IN SIGHT!

WITH A LOUD PING, ORSIPPE'S BELT FINALLY GAVE WAY. HIS LEGS BUCKLED. HIS SHORTS SLIPPED DOWN TO HIS ANKLES. MOMENTS LATER HE TRIPPED OVER THEM! ALL HE COULD DO WAS LIE FLAT ON HIS FACE AS THE OTHER RUNNERS SURGED PAST.

'THEY ALL LAUGHED AT ME' SAID ORSIPPES AFTER THE RACE. 'WHAT A CHEEK!'

HE SOUNDED VERY SORE ABOUT THINGS - NOT TOO SURPRISING CONSIDERING THE RESULT HAD LEFT HIM IN BOTTOM POSITION!

THE SAME THING WILL NEVER HAPPEN AGAIN, THOUGH. FROM NOW ON, COMPETITORS WILL WEAR ONLY A HELMET AND CARRY A SHIELD. THEY WILL **NOT** WEAR SHORTS AT ALL.

AS ONE OFFICIAL TOLD ME: 'NEXT TIME, WHEN THE RACE STARTS AND THE CROWD SHOUT 'THEY'RE OFF!" IT'LL MEAN JUST THAT.'

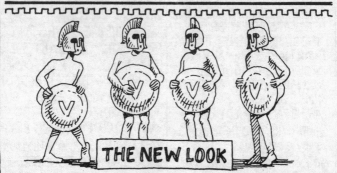

THE NEW LOOK

This actually happened to a runner once during the 'running-in-armour' race at the ancient Games. After that they did away with shorts and the rest, the runners only wearing a helmet and carrying a shield. Obviously they couldn't 'bare' the thought of it happening again!

Did you know...

About these athletes who also insisted on wearing the right gear?

● **Herb Elliott** of Australia, who won the 1500 m gold medal in 1960, wore running shoes made of kangaroo hide. They certainly put a spring in his step – he won every 1500 m race he ever ran!

● **Abebe Bikila** of Ethiopia, on the other foot, didn't wear running shoes at all when he won the 1960 marathon. Maybe that's how he managed to show the other runners a clean pair of heels!

● **Cathy Freeman** of Australia worried her whole nation as she lined up for the Sydney 2000 women's 400 m final wearing a shimmering silver head-to-toe jump suit. Would the colour be an unlucky omen? They needn't have worried. Freeman stayed one jump ahead of her opponents throughout the race and turned silver into gold.

● **Jacky Joyner-Kersee** of the USA, heptathlon champion in 1988 and 1992, always wore her sports bra. She suffered from asthma and kept her inhaler inside it!

All a bit different from one runner, who did quite the opposite in 1896 and wore something he never usually wore. Realizing that King George I of Greece would be watching, French sprinter Alphonse Grisel wore white gloves out of politeness because he was running in front of royalty. He didn't win a medal, but when it came to style – you had to hand it to him!

So, you've trained and trained, you've eaten all the right food and you're wearing all the right gear – now comes the big question. What event are you going in for?

SCORCHING PERFORMANCES – SUPERSTARS AND SIZZLING SPECTATORS

The Olympic Games are a bit like a school timetable. New subjects come in, and others go out (usually the ones you like!). Deciding which sports are in or out of the Olympics is the job of the International Olympic Committee (IOC). They try to be fair to everybody. Unlike the Emperor Nero when he took over the ancient Games…

RIGHT, I WANT SOME NEW EVENTS IN THIS YEAR'S GAMES!

ER… WHAT SORT OF EVENTS, EMPEROR?

THINGS I'M BRILLIANT AT, OF COURSE! LIKE SINGING. AND ACTING. AND I WANT A TEN-HORSE CHARIOT RACE, AS WELL.

BUT NOBODY ELSE HAS A TEN-HORSE CHARIOT.

This scandal took place in AD 67 and – surprise, surprise! – Nero won all the events he went in for. He even won the chariot race after being thrown out of his ten-horse chariot and not finishing the race! His name isn't in the record book any more though. When the nutty Emperor was persuaded to commit suicide a year later, the Games were declared invalid and the judges made to pay the money back.

Medals, medals, medals

Events in the modern Olympics have changed quite a lot. We saw in Chapter Three the different sports that will be played in the 2016 Games. Here's the complete list, with the total number of 306 gold medals up for grabs. Which sports do you think were in the first modern Games 100 years ago?

SPORT	MEDALS TO BE WON
AQUATICS	46, DIVIDED BETWEEN INDIVIDUAL AND TEAM EVENTS
ARCHERY	4
ATHLETICS	47, DIVIDED BETWEEN TRACK AND FIELD EVENTS
BADMINTON	5
BASKETBALL	2 TEAM MEDALS
BOXING	13. 1 FOR EACH WEIGHT DIVISION (10 MEN, 3 WOMEN)
CANOE/KAYAK	16
CYCLING	18 DIVIDED BETWEEN TRACK, ROAD AND CROSS-COUNTRY RACING
EQUESTRIAN	6, DIVIDED BETWEEN INDIVIDUAL AND TEAM EVENTS
FENCING	10
FOOTBALL	2 TEAM MEDALS

SPORT	MEDALS TO BE WON
GOLF	2
GYMNASTICS	18, DIVIDED BETWEEN INDIVIDUAL AND TEAM EVENTS
HANDBALL	2 TEAM MEDALS
HOCKEY	2 TEAM MEDALS
JUDO	14
MOD. PENTATHLON	2
ROWING	14
RUGBY SEVENS	2
SAILING	10
SHOOTING	15
TABLE TENNIS	4, SINGLES AND TEAM
TAEKWONDO	8, IN 4 WEIGHT DIVISIONS
TENNIS	5, SINGLES AND DOUBLES
TRIATHLON	2
VOLLEYBALL	4, 2 FOR BEACH, 2 FOR INDOOR
WEIGHTLIFTING	15
WRESTLING	18

Future events?

Before a new event is allowed in to the Olympics, it has to be 'recognized' by the IOC. These are the rules:

- for a *men's event*: it has to be widely played in at least 75 countries on 4 continents.
- for a *women's event*: it has to be widely played in at least 40 countries on 3 continents.

What's that? Games like 'tag' and 'hopscotch' qualify? They probably do, but there's more. The sport has to be officially run in every one of those countries, and then is only allowed in to the Games after some complicated voting. So, no 'tag' or 'hopscotch' – but that still leaves a fair number of sports which could be added at some stage. Which of these are recognized by the IOC and are therefore possible future events?

a) Ballroom Dancing
b) Baseball
c) Chess
d) Kitesurfing
e) Netball
f) Squash
g) Tenpin bowling

Extinct events

Quite a few sports have been in the Olympics – and then out again. Here are some flaming facts about some of them:

Obstacle race

This was a 200 m race. Here's what you had to do between the start and finish lines:

- climb over a pole
- scramble over a row of upturned boats
- scramble *under* a row of upturned boats

Not easy, eh? Oh yes, one other thing. The track the race was run on was:

- the River Seine

Yes, it was a swimming race! It only appeared in the Paris games of 1900, then went down the plug-hole.

Rugby

Although rugby sevens will feature in Rio 2106, full 15-man rugby hasn't been seen since the 1924 Paris Olympics. Why not? Probably because of the blood-soaked final, in which USA beat France 17 – 3. When the French team's star player, Adolph Jaureguy, was carried off injured after just two minutes the home fans rioted. They threw bottles and rocks on the pitch and the USA's Gideon Nelson was knocked out by a spectator's walking stick! If 7-person rugby only causes half the trouble of 15-person it'll still be worth watching!

Standing long jump

Until 1912, there were standing high and long jump events. The idea was that you jumped from where you were, rather than taking a run-up. The absolute star at this was the American Ray Ewry, who won a total of eight gold medals. His success was all down to his doctor. Ewry suffered from rheumatic fever and the doctor's prescription told him to take up running and jumping to get his strength back.

Try the standing long jump! Here's how:

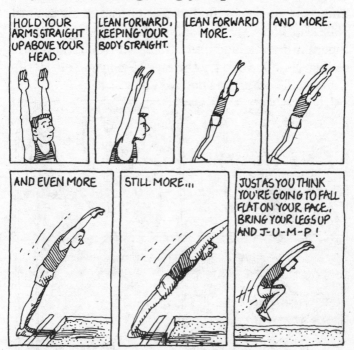

HOLD YOUR ARMS STRAIGHT UP ABOVE YOUR HEAD.	LEAN FORWARD, KEEPING YOUR BODY STRAIGHT.	LEAN FORWARD MORE.	AND MORE.
AND EVEN MORE	STILL MORE...		JUST AS YOU THINK YOU'RE GOING TO FALL FLAT ON YOUR FACE, BRING YOUR LEGS UP AND J-U-M-P!

YOU'VE ALREADY FALLEN FLAT ON YOUR FACE? TOUGH. GO BACK TO STEP 1. WHEN YOU CAN JUMP 3·33 METRES YOU'LL BE AS GOOD AS RAY EWRY.

Tug-of-war

This was stopped in 1920 but it had its moments.

In 1908, the Liverpool Police were representing Great Britain and they beat a USA team in seconds. The Americans lodged a protest, saying that the policemen had special boots with spikes, steel cleats and heels. The police argued, saying the boots weren't special at all. They were the boots they wore every day on the beat!

Rope climb

This was an event in the gymnastics section until 1932. The idea is pretty simple. Find a length of strong rope ten metres long and attach it to your classroom ceiling. Now you can try the rope climb yourself. Here's a simple flowchart to show you how:

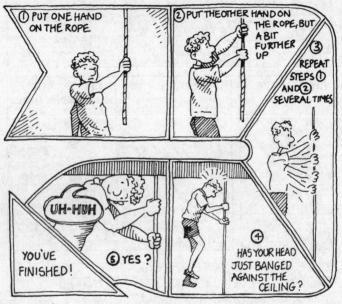

Raymond Bass of the USA was the last winner of a rope-climbing gold medal. He did the ten metres in 6.7 seconds!

Olympic ode-ity!

Great Britain won a gold medal in 1896 for an event that didn't exist – and never has! A scholar, Sir George Robertson, read an ode (a poem) praising the Greek king. The king was so delighted he awarded Robertson an honorary medal!

The mind-boggling marathon

The marathon is probably the most famous event in the whole of the Olympic games. It's a running race which commemorates the run a Greek messenger called Pheidippides is supposed to have made in 490 BC. In those days they didn't have postboxes or post vans. So, if somebody wanted to send a letter, they:

1. wrote it

2. stuck it in an envelope

3. put an address on the front

4. gave the envelope to somebody like Pheidippedes

5. said, "Get going, Pheidippedes. You're supposed to be a first-class male!"

This is just what happened on the day in question. The Greeks had defeated the Persians in a battle on the Plain of Marathon and Pheidippedes' boss, Miltiades, wanted everybody in their home city of Athens to know about his triumph as soon as possible.

The trouble was, Athens was a bit far off – like, 280 km kind of far off. Still, Pheidippedes did his best. He galloped away, but by the time he reached his destination he wasn't feeling too bright. In fact he just about had enough strength left to cry, "Rejoice! We conquer!" before he collapsed and died. (If he'd done the same thing today he might have said "Flaming Olympics!" instead.)

The marathon isn't run over 280 km nowadays, though. It's run over the most curious distance of 26 miles and 385 yards (42.2 km).

It wasn't always this distance. In 1896 the marathon was a 25-mile race (40.2 km). Then, in 1908, the Olympics were held in London and somebody thought it would be a good idea for the race to start at Windsor Castle. Inconveniently, Windsor Castle was 26 miles from the White City stadium, not 25 miles. Then, so the story goes, Princess Mary asked if the poor old runners could do another 385 yards so that they finished underneath the Royal box. And everybody agreed! The 26 miles and 385 yards marathon was born.

92

Make your own 'the marathon' board game

Actually running a marathon is pretty hard. So, why not do it the easy way and make your own marathon board game to play instead? That way you'll get all the thrills but none of the agony. You'll need: one dice and a board 26 miles 385 yards (42.195 km) long.

The idea is to take it in turns to throw the dice, moving yourself along the board by the appropriate number of spaces.

So first you've got to divide the board into 46,145 squares (one for each yard). Then, to make life interesting, put in the following penalty squares based on things that have really happened in Olympic marathons.

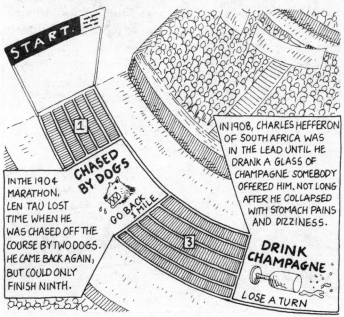

START.

1

CHASED BY DOGS

GO BACK 1 MILE

IN THE 1904 MARATHON, LEN TAU LOST TIME WHEN HE WAS CHASED OFF THE COURSE BY TWO DOGS. HE CAME BACK AGAIN, BUT COULD ONLY FINISH NINTH.

3

IN 1908, CHARLES HEFFERON OF SOUTH AFRICA WAS IN THE LEAD UNTIL HE DRANK A GLASS OF CHAMPAGNE. SOMEBODY OFFERED HIM. NOT LONG AFTER HE COLLAPSED WITH STOMACH PAINS AND DIZZINESS.

DRINK CHAMPAGNE

LOSE A TURN

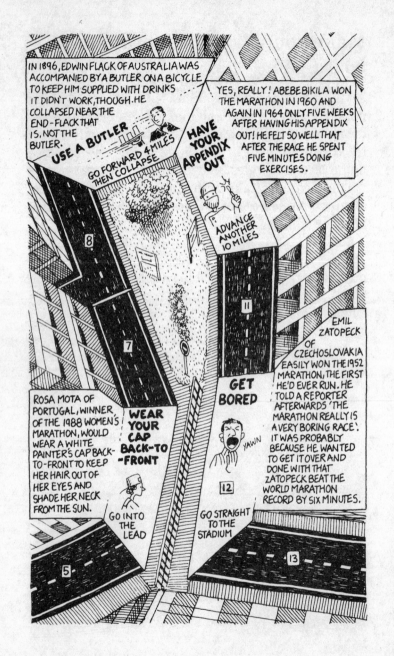

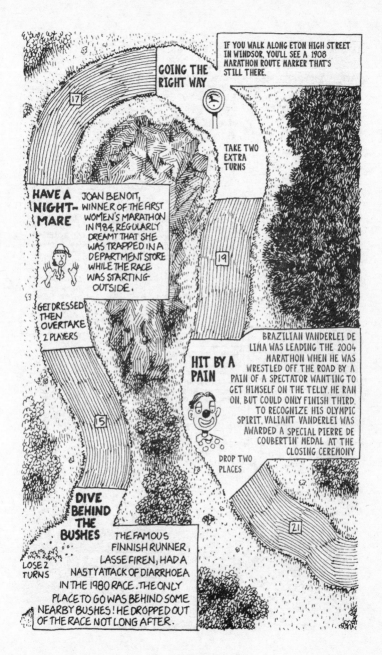

GOING THE RIGHT WAY

17

IF YOU WALK ALONG ETON HIGH STREET IN WINDSOR, YOU'LL SEE A 1908 MARATHON ROUTE MARKER THAT'S STILL THERE.

TAKE TWO EXTRA TURNS

19

HAVE A NIGHT-MARE

JOAN BENOIT, WINNER OF THE FIRST WOMEN'S MARATHON IN 1984, REGULARLY DREAMT THAT SHE WAS TRAPPED IN A DEPARTMENT STORE WHILE THE RACE WAS STARTING OUTSIDE.

GET DRESSED THEN OVERTAKE 2 PLAYERS

5

HIT BY A PAIN

BRAZILIAN VANDERLEI DE LIMA WAS LEADING THE 2004 MARATHON WHEN HE WAS WRESTLED OFF THE ROAD BY A PAIN OF A SPECTATOR WANTING TO GET HIMSELF ON THE TELLY. HE RAN ON, BUT COULD ONLY FINISH THIRD. TO RECOGNIZE HIS OLYMPIC SPIRIT, VALIANT VANDERLEI WAS AWARDED A SPECIAL PIERRE DE COUBERTIN' MEDAL AT THE CLOSING CEREMONY

DROP TWO PLACES

21

DIVE BEHIND THE BUSHES

LOSE 2 TURNS

THE FAMOUS FINNISH RUNNER, LASSE FIREN, HAD A NASTY ATTACK OF DIARRHOEA IN THE 1980 RACE. THE ONLY PLACE TO GO WAS BEHIND SOME NEARBY BUSHES! HE DROPPED OUT OF THE RACE NOT LONG AFTER.

95

IN THE 1904 MARATHON, FRED LORZ OF THE USA WAS FIRST MAN OUT OF THE STADIUM AT THE START AND FIRST MAN IN AGAIN AT THE FINISH, LOOKING AS THOUGH HE'D HARDLY RUN AT ALL. THIS WAS BECAUSE HE'D HARDLY RUN AT ALL! AFTER GETTING CRAMP, FRED HAD HITCHED A LIFT BACK IN A CAR. AS THEY GOT NEAR THE STADIUM THE CAR BROKE DOWN. BUT BY THEN SNEAKY FRED WAS FEELING BETTER. SO HE GOT OUT AND RAN THE LAST BIT TO THE FINISHING LINE! HE WAS BANNED FOR LIFE.

CAUGHT CHEATING

25

OUT OF THE GAME AND NOT ALLOWED TO PLAY AGAIN

THE 1908 MARATHON IN LONDON WAS RUN IN HOT, HUMID WEATHER. BY THE TIME HE GOT TO THE STADIUM THE LEADER, THE TINY DORANDO PIETRI OF ITALY, WAS SO EXHAUSTED HE TWICE COLLAPSED ON THE TRACK. IN THE END HE HAD TO BE HELPED OVER THE LINE BY AN OFFICIAL — AND WAS PROMPTLY DISQUALIFIED! QUEEN ALEXANDRA FELT SO SORRY FOR HIM THAT SHE AWARDED HIM HIS OWN CUP AS A CONSOLATION PRIZE.

YOU'RE EXHAUSTED

LET 2 PLAYERS OVERTAKE YOU.

IN THE 1948 RACE, ETIENNE GAILLY WAS IN THE LEAD AS HE ENTERED THE STADIUM WITH ONLY A FEW HUNDRED YARDS TO GO. BUT HE WAS SO EXHAUSTED HE WAS PASSED BY TWO OTHER RUNNERS BEFORE HE COULD GET TO THE FINISHING LINE.

GIVEN A HAND

DISQUALIFIED BUT AWARDED A CONSOLATION PRIZE

GET SUNSTROKE

FRANCISCO LAZARO OF PORTUGAL DIED OF SUNSTROKE IN 1912

23

OUT OF THE GAME

IN 1912, THE JAPANESE RUNNER SHIZO KANAKURI DROPPED OUT OF THE RACE WITH HEAT EXHAUSTION. HE VOWED THAT HE'D FINISH THE RACE ONE DAY — AND HE DID. IN 1967 HE WENT BACK TO THE OLYMPIC STADIUM IN STOCKHOLM AND RAN A FINAL LAP. SO HIS TIME FOR THE RACE WAS 54 YEARS, 2 DAYS, 32 MINUTES AND 20.3 SECONDS.

RETIRE EXHAUSTED

WAIT 54 YEARS FOR YOUR NEXT THROW.

22

FINISH!

96

The marathon game prize

The first player to get to the line is the winner. Of course, this being an Olympics game, you should give the winner a gold medal. You might like to come up with a few other prizes as well...

Question: In the first modern Games, held in Athens, the Greeks hadn't won a single athletics gold medal. By the time it came to the final event, the marathon, they were getting desperate. Offers of prizes came in from all over the country. So, which of these prizes did various Greeks offer to any of their countrymen who could win the 1896 marathon?
a) A barrel of wine.
b) 900 kg of chocolate.
c) Free shaves for life.
d) Marriage to a daughter, plus one million drachmas.
e) Free clothing for life.

Answer: all of them!

A Greek named Spiridon Louis promptly won the race – and turned down all the prizes. His job was transporting fresh water to Athens, so he asked for a horse and cart instead!

97

Flaming spectators

The stars of the Olympics are the competitors. But sometimes spectators can't resist joining in with the action themselves...

The sporty Spartan

It happened in the ancient Olympics of course. Lichas, a Spartan, desperately wanted to win the chariot-race (the owner of the chariot and horses was proclaimed the winner, remember, not the chariot driver). The trouble was, Spartans weren't being allowed into the Games that year. So Lichas entered his chariot team under a false name and turned up to watch as a spectator.

So far, so good – until Lichas's team won the race. He couldn't contain his delight. Instead of staying undercover as a spectator, he charged across to the judges and claimed his prize. Twit. The judges spotted he was a Spartan at once. Instead of the laurel wreath he wanted, Lichas got a flogging instead.

Norbert the nuisance

Like Lichas, Norbert Sudhous couldn't resist being part of the action either. His moment of 'fame' came in 1972.

He was in the Olympic stadium. All around him, the crowd were eagerly awaiting the arrival of the leading runner in the marathon. So what did Norbert do? While everybody was looking the other way he...

- took off his jumper
- took off his shirt
- took off his trousers leaving him, in his vest and underpants, looking a bit like a runner. So next he...
- jumped out on the track, and...
- ran round pretending to be an athlete!

The crowd didn't realize for a while, and applauded him loudly as he ran most of the way round the track. Then, when they did realize, they booed him loudly. Finally the stadium guards grabbed Norbert and carried him away. They got the loudest cheer of all!

WHAT AN UNDIE-HAND TRICK!

Graffiti vandal

In 2004 one proud parent didn't get off the starting line at all. The night before British cyclist Nicole Cooke's road race, her father Anthony crept out armed with a brush and a pot of white paint. His plan was to write Nicole's name on the road in the hope that she'd be inspired every time she rode over it. But before he'd finished along came the Greek police and arrested him!

The paddling papa

Another spectator went even further in 1952. Jean Boiteaux of France had just won the 400 m freestyle when there was an almighty splash at the other end of the pool. A spectator had leapt in – not undressed, like Norbert Sudhous, but fully clothed! He'd even left his french beret on.

Before anybody could stop him, the spectator swam strongly across to Boiteaux. What did the new champion do? He took it all very calmly. He allowed the spectator to kiss him on both cheeks, then helped him out of the pool.

Surprising? Not really. The spectator was Boiteaux's father who'd seen his son's victory and just couldn't wait to congratulate him.

These were all spectators who were supposed to have stayed in the crowd. Once, though, a spectator was actually asked to come out from the crowd and join in with the competition. It happened on 26 August, 1900...

The super-sub

"Papa," said the young boy, seeing his father putting on his hat and coat, "where are you going?"

"To the river, Philippe," said his father.

"Why?" asked Philippe. It was his favourite question.

His father smiled. "Because there are some rowing races taking place today."

"Why?"

"They are part of the Olympic Games, Philippe. The Games are being held here, in Paris."

"Why?"

"Oh, Philippe! Why not come with me and see for yourself?"

Philippe nodded eagerly and smiled happily at the same time. It always worked! If he asked enough questions, his father would suggest he came with him just to get some peace.

He skipped along as his father led the way from their small house and down to the banks of the River Seine. On this pleasant August day, the mighty river which ran right through Paris was smooth and calm.

Other people were hurrying in the same direction. Philippe looked out across the river.

"See the flags, Philippe?" said his father, pointing out at the rows of gaily-coloured flags dotted about on the water.

"What are they doing?" said Philippe, asking his second-favourite question.

"They are marking out the course for the rowing boats to follow."

Even as he said it, they heard the crash of the starter's gun. "Look, Philippe!" shouted the boy's father. "There they are!"

In the distance, away down the river, Philippe could just make out the three small rowing boats coming towards them. Each had two persons rowing, bending their backs as they pulled their oars strongly through the water. Each boat also had another person in it.

"That third one isn't rowing," said Philippe. He suddenly realized he hadn't used his favourite question for some time. "Why?"

"He is called the cox," said his father. "He doesn't row at all. His job is to steer the boat."

"An easy job, if you ask me!" said Philippe. "I could do that!" He had steered his father's small rowing boat on the river many a time.

They watched as the two leading boats went by, little between them. "I think it will be between those two in the final," said the boy's father. He began to move along the bank towards the finishing line. "Come on. Let's see them when they pull their boats from the water."

Philippe followed, dodging between the people going the same way. When they reached the finishing line, he ducked and weaved a bit more until he was at the front of the crowd.

"Here is the Dutch boat," his father said from behind him. "They came second. And they don't look too happy about it."

Philippe could see that for himself. The two rowers were shaking their heads and looking back angrily at the cox.

"He is too fat!" one was saying. "He slowed us down."

"I agree," said the other Dutch rower. "We will be second in the final too, unless we do something about it."

The first rower looked at his partner. "What?"

"Get him to lose some weight!" said the second rower, jerking a thumb towards their cox.

"Impossible! The final is this afternoon!"

"Then there's only one thing to do," said the first rower. "Find ourselves another cox."

"Another cox?"

"Yes, another cox. Somebody light! Somebody who can steer straight!"

The rowers looked at each other in despair. They shook their heads. It was hopeless. And then they heard a little voice from the front of the crowd.

"I'm light," said Philippe. "And I can steer straight."

After coming second in the heats, the two-man Dutch crew in the 1900 Olympic coxed pairs event changed their cox, Hermanus Brockman, for the final because they'd decided he was too heavy. In his place they used a French boy, taken from the spectators. The boy's name isn't known but he was between seven and ten years old and is the youngest-ever Olympic gold medal winner. With him as their cox, the Dutch team won the final by just 0.2 seconds!

Gotcha!
Finally, the tale of two spectators who wished they'd not bothered.

A couple of Brazilian volleyball fans were desperate to see their country's volleyball team compete in the 1992 Olympics in Barcelona. So, off they went to the stadium. The TV cameras were there, of course, beaming pictures back to those watching on TV in Brazil.

During a pause in the match, the cameras turned to show the faces in the crowd ... and the two fans were arrested shortly after. They were wanted crooks, who'd fled from Brazil owing £10 million!

Pass!

Volunteers (they were called Games Makers) who helped out at the London 2012 Games were supplied with:

• Two purple and red shirts
• two pairs of grey trousers
• two pairs of socks
• one jacket
• one pair of trainers
• an umbrella, a water bottle, a notepad ...
• and a bag to put it all in.

Most important, though, was their identity pass, to ensure they were allowed in. It was worn round their necks and, to ensure that they didn't lose it, volunteers were encouraged to keep it on at all times!

PLAYING WITH FIRE – CHAMPION CHEATS

Athletes like to win (don't we all?) but some – and it's only a few – want to win so much that they'll try anything they can to gain an advantage. It's called cheating, and it's been going on since competitions began. The Greek poet, Homer, says even the Greek gods did it!

ODYSSEUS IS HAVING A RACE WITH AJAX. IT'S NECK AND NECK.
"OH, DEARSEUS," THINKS ODYSSEUS, "WHAT CAN I DO?" THERE'S ONLY ONE THING HE CAN THINK OF DOING, SO HE DOES IT. HE PRAYS TO THE GODDESS ATHENA FOR HELP.
"ATHENA, POLE-AXE THIS AJAX!"

LO AND BEHOLD (OR, RATHER, LOW AND BEHOLD) AJAX PROMPTLY SLIDES FACE FIRST INTO A PILE OF OX DUNG! ODYSSEUS WINS THE RACE!

A rather dirty trick, wouldn't you say? And all Ajax could do afterwards was become a little cleaner! (If you don't get this joke, ask your mum.)

Following this good example, trickery and skulduggery went on at the ancient Games too. Even though the athletes promised to play fair at the opening ceremony, they still regularly practised these friendly little tricks. Can you match them with the event in which they were used?

a) Tripping and shoving as you went round the turning post.

1. Pankration

b) Rubbing sand in your opponent's eyes.

2. Chariot race

c) Biting

3. Foot races

d) Bribing the judges to make you the winner even if you fall out and don't actually finish the race.

4. Wrestling

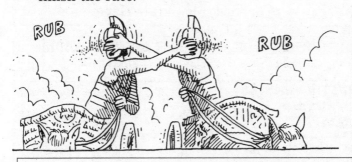

RUB   RUB

Answers: a) 3. (a trick which sent runners round the bend when it happened to them.); **b)** 4. (as practised by particularly gritty performers); **c)** 1. (otherwise known as teething troubles); **d)** 2. (a speciality of the Emperor Nero, proving yet again what a big fiddler he was).

And that's the way it's been during the whole history of the modern Olympics, too. Competitors have carried on playing tricks to help them win. Some of the tricks have been sneaky, some have been mean, some have been dirty – and some have been sneaky, mean *and* dirty! Here are a few...

Bribery

As usual, the ancient Olympics led the way in this. Without any TV cameras taking close-ups or photo-finishes, decisions were all down to the judges. So bribing a judge to say you'd won your race was one way of winning. The other way was to bribe your opponent. The earliest case of this took place in 388 BC when a boxer named Eupolus bribed three other boxers to let him win.

What was the punishment for somebody who was found guilty of bribery?

a) They paid a fine.
b) They were banned from future Games.
c) They received a flogging.
d) Their title and wreath were taken away if they'd won their event.

IT'S THE WINNERS WHIPPING SESSION!

Answer: a) or **b)** or **c)** could be right, but **d)** is definitely wrong! Amazingly, somebody who'd used bribery to win their event wasn't disqualified but allowed to remain the winner!

Usually the cheat had to pay a fine, the money being used to erect a statue to Zeus. On the bottom would be a message saying something like: "Olympic champions win with speed and strength, not money." This sounds pretty good, but as the cheat was still allowed to remain the winner it also sounds pretty daft!

Here comes the judge!

There have been cases in the modern Olympics where the judges haven't needed to be bribed, they've volunteered to cheat (well, not exactly cheat perhaps – just not stick to the rules)! At the opening ceremony the judges promise not to take sides. But what would you say these did...

● In the 1908 middleweight boxing final, Reg Baker (Australia) accused the judge of being biased towards the winner, John Douglas (Britain). The judge denied it ... even though his surname was Douglas and he was the winner's father!

● Another famous case occurred in 1952, at the end of the 10 km walk. In a tight finish for second place a Swiss, Fritz Schwab, and a Russian, Bruno Yunk, were neck and neck (well, toe and toe). They got faster ... and faster ... until, 30 m from the line they forget all about walking and started running. But the judges (who were anti-Russian) said everything had been fine and Schwab had won the silver medal fairly – even though both 'walkers' had outsprinted the judges to the finishing line!

● Things hadn't improved by 1988 in Seoul, where an amazingly high number of South Korean boxers managed to score wins. After one final, in which Park Si-Hun of South Korea was judged to have beaten Roy Jones (USA), a number of the judges were suspended. Jones was later awarded a cup as the best boxer in the Games

● In 2004, American gymnast Paul Hamm bounced away with the gold medal because his nearest rival, Korean Yang Tae Young, was accidentally given a lower score then he should have received. Three judges were suspended – one of them American, another a Columbian who worked in the USA. Even then the decision might have been altered ... but the Korean team didn't lodge their protest until long after the gymnastics had finished! So, what's an athlete to do if he thinks he's been cheated? In 2008, taekwondo fighter Angel Matos from Cuba took the law into his own hands – or, rather, his own feet. When the referee disqualified him during his bronze-medal match, not-so-angelic Angel showed what he thought of the decision. He gave the referee a perfect taekwondo-style kick in the face! Bad move. The outraged officials kicked back. Miserable Matos was banned for life.

False starts

The most common type of cheating in a running race is the false start – that is, trying to get away before the starter's gun goes off.

What punishment did you receive if you were guilty of a false start at the ancient Games?

a) You had to pay a fine.

b) You were banned from future Games.

c) You received a flogging.

d) Your title and wreath were taken away if you'd won your event.

Answer: c) Yes, in those days the punishment fitted the crime. If you'd beaten the starter, the starter had you beaten!

Nowadays the rule is one false start and you're out. This has changed over the years, though. Until 2003 only your second false start counted. And back in 1904 a runner had to go back by about 2 metres for every false start he made. This was dead handy for the USA sprinter Archie Hahn. There were three other runners in his race – and they all had false starts, one after the other! Hahn won the gold medal.

111

Sometimes, though, the judges have a tricky decision to make. See if you can get this one right. It happened to a Russian named Rapp in the 1,000 m cycling time trial in 1972…

1. Before the pistol went, Rapp started moving.

2. Realizing he'd made a false start, and thinking he'd be ordered to start again, Rapp stopped.

What happened next?

> **Answer:** Rapp was disqualified – but not for the false start. The judges hadn't spotted that, so they disqualified Rapp for stopping. (A clear case of an innocent man taking the Rapp for something he didn't do!)

Punch-ups

Fighting your opponent is sometimes allowed – but not when you're supposed to be in a running race! In the ancient Games, though, it happened all the time. The runners in the 2 stade and 24 stade races didn't have to stay in lanes or anything like that, they just had to charge down the track and go round the posts which were positioned at each end. Take your pick from this list of what runners weren't supposed to do to each other – but did!

- Tripping (another one bites the dust!)

- Holding (nasty, they were all naked remember)

- Running in front of somebody (so that he ran into the post)

- Going inside, not outside, the post (first example of taking a short cut)

I say, that's not British!

Believe it or not, a similar problem occurred in the 1908 Games 400 m race. At that time there were no lanes round the track at White City Stadium in London. Four runners were in the race, three from the USA and one, Wyndham Halswelle, from Britain. As they hit the final straight it was neck and neck between Halswelle and Carpenter, one of the Americans. As Halswelle tried to overtake, Carpenter moved out and blocked his path. After an objection, the race was run again.

What do you think happened in the re-run?

a) Carpenter won.

b) Halswelle won.

c) Neither of them won.

Answer: b) Halswelle won – running on his own! Carpenter refused to run again, and the other two Americans did the same. In the history of Olympic athletics, this is the only time there's been a walk-over. (Why not a run-over?) Ever since, the running track has been divided into lanes all the way round and runners can't leave their lane.

Even more punch-ups

The events in which punch-ups are supposed to take place still give plenty of opportunities for cheating, though. Which of these were boxers allowed to do in the ancient Games, and which are they allowed to do now?

a) Hitting the back of the neck (called a rabbit punch, because it's the method used to kill a rabbit).

b) Hitting below the belt.

c) Hitting with the heel of the hand.

d) Hitting a man on the ground.

e) Hitting with the teeth (biting, in other words!).

f) Gouging – that is, poking your thumb in the other man's eye and pulling it out (your thumb and his eye!).

Answers: Boxing in the ancient Games allowed **a) b) c)** and **d)**, but not **e)** and **f)**. In modern boxing, none of them are allowed.

"Tell that to the judge!" might have been the cry of Harry Mallin, in 1924. He was defending his middleweight title against a Frenchman named Roger Brousse and lost on points. What did Mallin immediately claim that the Frenchman had done to him during the fight?

a) Kissed him on both cheeks.

b) Whispered rude words in his ear.

c) Bitten him on the chest.

Answer: c) Whereupon the judges examined Mallin's chest and found the teethmarks. Mallin was awarded the fight and went on to win the gold medal again.

How about this one, concerning two French cyclists? In the 1936 cycling road race over 100 km, Guy Lapebie was just in front of Robert Charpentier as they raced for the finishing line. Suddenly, Lapebie slowed down – and Charpentier went past him to win by a fraction of a second. What had happened to Lapebie?

a) Wheel trouble.

b) Back trouble.

c) Pedal trouble.

Answer: b) Charpentier had grabbed his shirt, and pulled him back!

Fixing the equipment

In the ancient Games it was a case of fixing the judges or your opponents. Nowadays, with the arrival of timing equipment and cameras, it's not so easy to cheat. But some have tried...

Glow home, Boris!

In fencing, for instance, a lot of the judging is done electronically. Fencers wear breastplates which are wired up, as are their swords. This way, when one fencer's sword hits the other's breastplate a light on the judges' table comes on.

Boris Onyschenko, a Russian, tried to fix the equipment in 1976. His aim was to fool the judges into thinking he'd scored a hit when he hadn't. The trouble was, he fixed things too well. The light came on before he'd got near enough to reach his opponent! What happened to him? He was told to "glow" home, of course!

116

Getting a grip on things

In another famous case, the equipment got fixed later. Harold Osborn (USA), the winner of the 1924 high jump, had a very interesting technique. It was:

1. run in;

2. take off;

3. use a hand to press the bar back against the high-jump post so that it didn't fall off if he whacked it on the way over;

4. land.

117

He managed a (then) Olympic record leap of 1.98 metres using this method – which wasn't against the rules. Afterwards, though, the design of the high jump posts was changed so that the pegs on which the bar rested were inside them, rather than at the back of them. Osborn's technique couldn't be used any more.

Pills and potions

In the history of the modern Games, plenty of competitors have been caught taking drugs to make their performance better.

Many of them have been weightlifters and wrestlers, who take drugs to give them extra strength. Some have been taking part in shooting events, using drugs that would calm their nerves and keep their hands steady. Others, such as cyclists and runners, use drugs to gain extra power and speed.

In their desire to win, they ignore the dangers of taking drugs. And the dangers are very real. In the 1960 Games, the Danish cyclist Knut Jensen died because of the drugs he'd taken.

Of all the drugs cases, though, none caused more of a scandal than that of the Canadian sprinter Ben Johnson in 1988. In the 100 m final Johnson had rocketed from his starting blocks to win the race in a world-record time, his arch-rival Carl Lewis (USA) beaten into second place.

Johnson received his gold medal and, like all medalists, was drugs-tested. His test proved that he'd been taking drugs called steroids, to give him extra power. Johnson was immediately disqualified and his gold medal awarded to Lewis.

He had been the fastest man in the world for only two days.

Flaming Fact

Until the Olympics returned to Greece in 2004, Ben Johnson was the only athlete ever to have been stripped of his gold medal for taking drugs. But by the end of the Games he'd been joined by three more. The most disgraceful was that of the Russian Irina Korzhanenko who failed a drugs test after winning the women's shot-put. Not only had her event taken place at the sacred site at Olympia, it was the very first event of the Games – less than twenty-four hours after the athlete's oath at the opening ceremony!

Who, me...?

The rules about drugs are very strict, and sometimes athletes can take them almost without knowing.

The swimmer Rick Demont (USA) was disqualified after winning the 400 m freestyle in 1972, even though he hadn't deliberately taken drugs. He was an asthma sufferer, and the drug was in the inhalant he used.

It's pretty dumb for an athlete to take drugs anyway, but it's doubly dumb when they don't help at all! The oldest Olympic competitor to be caught taking drugs so far has been Paul Cerutti of Monaco, who was 65 years old when he took part in the 1972 trap shooting event. He was disqualified, of course, although it didn't affect the result. He'd come 43rd out of 44!

When you've got to go, you've got to go!

Drug-taking is a serious business, but it does have its funny side.

Imagine you've just won an Olympic gold medal. This is what happens with a drugs test.

① YOU RETURN TO THE CHANGING-ROOM.

WELL DONE! NUMBER ONE!

② HE'S HOLDING AN EMPTY BOTTLE.

RIGHT LET'S HAVE A NUMBER ONE IN HERE AS WELL THEN!

What's more the official won't go away until he's got what he came for, however long you take between steps **3.** and **4.** Sometimes he's had rather a long wait though...

The boxing boozer

In 1968, Chris Finnegan (Britain) won the middle-weight boxing gold. Into the loo he went with his bottle – and didn't come out! He couldn't manage a drop! The officials sent out for a pint of beer. He still couldn't manage anything. They sent for another pint of beer ... and another ... and another ... Early next morning, Finnegan finally came out with something in his bottle. He'd had to drink eight pints!

The running dribbler

The runner Rod Dixon (New Zealand) had a similar problem after managing third place in the 1972 1,500 m race. After staying in the loo for some time, he sheepishly put his head round the door and handed out his bottle. It had the merest dribble in the bottom. "Will it do?" he asked. The official frowned, then finally nodded. "For a gold medal, no. But for a bronze, it will do."

The Finnish vampire

Drug-taking is about putting something false into your body to help you perform better. But what if you put some of your own blood into your body? Until 1984 this was allowed and the Finnish runner Lasse Viren was the most famous athlete accused of doing it. Here's how. (Readers, do not try this at home. It can make an awful mess in kitchen.)

- He was supposed to have taken 1 litre of blood (his own)...
- Put it in the freezer...
- Then had a lie down until his body had made enough new blood to fill him up again.

- Just before his next race, he'd taken the frozen blood out of the freezer (making sure it was his blood and not a bag of blackcurrent ice-lollies)...
- Defrosted it...
- Injected it back into his body...
- Then gone off and run his race.

BLOOD? I NEVER TOUCH THE STUFF!

This is called 'blood-boosting', and the idea is that, with an extra litre of blood inside you, your body will have far greater endurance than normal.

It sounds nasty, and Viren always denied that he used blood-boosting. The newspapers weren't so sure. They knew that the technique was developed in Viren's part of the world, and always thought it suspicious that he managed to be at his best for the major championships. Viren claimed it was good training.

Whatever the truth, he was certainly a brilliant athlete. Lasse Viren won both the 5,000 m and 10,000 m gold medals in 1972 and 1976.

Who are you – and WHAT are you?

Remember Kallipateira, the woman who sneaked in to watch the ancient Games dressed as a man because women weren't allowed? After this all competitors and trainers had to appear naked when they were entering events so that any woman posing as a man would be spotted at once!

In the modern Olympics, sex-testing as it is called, has been in force since 1968. But, unlike the Kallipateira case, it's not designed to reveal women pretending to be men, but the other way round – to discover women athletes who are really men. A lot of women object to this testing, saying that it is unfair and unnecessary. Against them, others argue that it makes sure everybody is equal.

Mind you, pretending to be a woman hasn't always been a good idea. At the 1936 Games a woman high-jumper named Dora Ratjen was found to be a man posing as a woman. It hadn't done him much good, though – he'd only come fourth!

124

Double Trouble

In 1984, though, one athlete fooled everybody about who she was. After injuring her ankle, Madeleine de Jesus (Puerto Rico) wasn't fit enough to run in the 4x400m relay. So she got her twin sister Margaret to do it instead!

Gamesmanship & sportsmanship

Question: When is cheating not cheating?

Answer: When it's gamesmanship! (Or gameswomanship – women do it just as well.)

Gamesmanship is doing something which is not against the rules but which puts your opponents off in some way, either by ruining their concentration or making them feel inferior in some way.

Zato the rat-o

The brilliant Czech runner Emil Zatopeck was really ace at this. In the 1952 marathon, the first he'd ever entered, he was well in the lead after 15 miles but slowed down to let Jim Peters (Britain) catch him up.

When Peters, who was one of the favourites to win the race, came gasping along, Zatopeck said to him:

I HAVEN'T RUN A MARATHON BEFORE, BUT... DON'T YOU THINK WE OUGHT TO GO FASTER?

And with that he shot off to win, leaving Peters feeling all petered out.

A good sport

Sportsmanship is the opposite to gamesmanship. It's doing something to make your opponent feel better, not worse – like the 800 m runner Earl Eby (USA) in 1920 who bumped into Rudd (South Africa) by accident and lost time by turning round to say "Sorry!"

The 'gamesman or sportsman?' test

So, are you a gamesman or a sportsman? Try this quiz to find out. All the questions are based on actual incidents that happened in the Olympics.

1. You're Harold Abrahams in 1924, and you've been entered for the 100 m and the long jump. You want to concentrate on the 100 m. What do you do?
a) Your best in both anyway.
b) Write a letter to the newspapers saying it was stupid picking you for the long jump, so that you can then show it to the people picking the team and ask to be excused.

2. You're Kenneth McCarthur, running with Christian Gilsham (both South Africa) in the 1912 marathon. He says he's going to stop for a drink at the next refreshment point. You say you'll wait for him. What do you do?
a) Wait for him, like you said.
b) Shoot off while he's having his drink.

I'LL JUST WAIT TEN MORE MINUTES!...

3. You're Lucien Duquesne of France, racing against Paavo Nurmi of Finland in the 1928 steeplechase. Nurmi has never run this race before and he falls at a hurdle. What do you do?

a) Stop and help him up.

b) Tread on him.

4. Now you're Nurmi, in the same race. It's the finishing straight, and you're neck and neck with Duquesne. What do you do?

a) Let him win because of what he did to you.

b) Try to beat the socks off him because of what he did to you.

5. You're Alistair Brownlee of Great Britain in 2012. Your great rival in the Triathlon, Javier Noya of Spain, is lying on the ground beside you gasping for breath. What do you do?

a) hold his hand.

b) give him the kiss of life.

6. You're Paavo Nurmi again, this time running in the 1920 10,000 m. What do you do?

a) Look at the other runners with respect.

b) Show you don't expect anybody else to keep up with you by carrying a stop-watch in your hand to see how fast you're going.

7. You're Joseph Guillemot (France), running in the same 1920 10,000 m race as Nurmi. He beats you. What do you do as you cross the finishing line?

a) Shake his hand.

b) Throw up all over him.

8. You're Ralph Craig, at the starting line for the 1912 100 m. False starts aren't allowed, but you don't get disqualified if you make one. What do you do?

a) Wait for the gun before moving.

b) Make as many false starts as you can to be sure of getting away well.

9. You're Luz Long of Germany, in the 1936 long jump. Your country's dictator, Adolf Hitler, has said you must beat Jesse Owens, a black American athlete. He's had two no-jumps. One more, and he's out of the competition. What do you do?

a) Give him some helpful advice.

b) Give him some unhelpful advice.

10. You're Bill Henry, the American stadium announcer at the 1932 Games in Los Angeles, USA. Lauri Lehtinen (Finland) has just beaten your country's runner, Ralph Hill, in the 5,000 m final after deliberately blocking him twice during the race. The crowd are booing. What do you do?

a) Ask the crowd to stop booing.

b) Join in, booing through your loudspeaker.

Answers:

1. b) Harold Abrahams (Britain) was chosen for both events in 1924. He wrote a letter to the Daily Express, didn't do the long jump – and won the 100 m.

2. b) McCarthur buzzed off – and won.

3. a) Duquesne stopped, helped Nurmi up and came second.

4. a) Nurmi allowed Duquesne to win.

5. a) Brownlee was gasping too. He'd just won gold, Noya silver. They shook hands laying down!

6. b) Nurmi did this in every race he ran, only throwing it infield when he started his final spurt for the finishing line.

7. b) To be fair, the race had been brought forward four hours at short notice and Guillemot had already eaten.

8. b) Craig had three false starts (nowadays he'd have been disqualified after two). He wasn't alone, though. There were seven false starts before the race was finally started for Craig to win.

9. a) Long suggested that Owen draw a line a few inches back from the take-off board and aim for that so as to be sure of getting in a good jump. Owens did as Long suggested, qualified for the final, and then won the gold medal with a world-record jump. Luz Long came second.

10. a) Henry quietened the crowd by saying, "Remember, these people are our guests."

How did you score?

*More **a)** than **b)*** You're a real sportsman.

*About equal **a)** and **b)*** You're a sport, but not all the time.

*More **b)** than **a)*** You need to be watched.

*All **b)*** I'd trust you as far as I could throw you with both hands tied behind my back!

Bananamanship!

The most curious accusation of gamesmanship was made at Atlanta in 1996, against the Malaysian badminton doubles pair of Cheah Soon Kit and Yap Kim Hock. They were supposed to have tried to get the upper hand of their opponents by bringing a bunch of green bananas on court to ward off evil spirits! If that was the idea, then they slipped up in the final – the Malaysians only won the silver medal.

BLAZING ROWS AND FLAMING OLYMPIC DISASTERS

In every competition there are winners and losers. But here are some Olympic competitors who didn't even get to take part! Try to guess why.

Miruts Yifter of Ethiopia turned up too late for his heat of the 5,000 m in 1972. Why?
1. He spent too long on the toilet.
2. He got lost.
3. He went to the wrong check-in gate stadium.

Answer: Nobody knows for sure, but it was rumoured to be all three! No wonder his nickname was Yifter the Shifter!

Wym Essajas of Surinam missed his 800 m first-round heat in 1960. Why?
1. He had a watch that stopped.
2. He got told the wrong time for his heat.
3. He spent too long in bed?

Answer: 2. and **3.** He was told his heat was in the afternoon, so he rested in the morning – which was when the race was really taking place. Essajas' disaster was a double. He was Surinam's first-ever competitor at the Olympics, and he had to go home without even running!

Ray Robinson and Eddie Hart (both USA) missed their 100 m semi-final in 1972. It was in the afternoon, not the evening as they thought. How did they find out the bad news?

1. They read about it in the evening newspaper.

2. They saw the race on a television.

3. They received a telephone call from the President of the United States.

Answer: 2. They saw it on a TV monitor as they waited for a bus to take them to the stadium. (They also read about it in the newspapers the next day, but it's a fair bet that the President didn't ring up to congratulate them!)

132

In 1976, 1980 and 1984 Mary Decker of the United States, was world-record holder and red-hot favourite for a 3,000 m gold medal but something stopped her. When did it happen?

1. 1976

2. 1980

3. 1984

Answer: All three! Mary Decker's luck was right out where the Olympics were concerned. In 1976 she was injured; in 1980 the USA team was withdrawn; and when she finally got to run in 1984 she tripped over Zola Budd in her first-round heat and failed to finish.

The unlucky thirteen

Mary Decker's disaster was just one of the many which litter Olympic history. They've been happening ever since that embarassed runner lost his shorts in the 'running-in-armour race' at the ancient Games (see page 78 for the bare facts!). His disaster, like Mary Decker's, was total. Neither of them managed to recover. Others have suffered disasters, though, and gone on to win medals.

See if you can work out what happened to the unlucky thirteen in this absolute disaster of a quiz!

1. The Cuban runner Feliz Carvajal set off for America in 1904. He wanted to run in the marathon, and he'd raised all his own money for the fare. **Disaster! What happened next?**

2. There was just 15 minutes to go before Charles

133

Vinci of the United States had his weight checked for the 1956 bantamweight section of the weightlifting. **Disaster!** He found he was 200 grams too heavy! **What happened next?**

3. Svante Rasmuson of Sweden needed to beat Masala of Italy in the 4,000 metres race, the last event of the 1984 modern pentathlon. On the last bend, Rasmuson was just ahead when ... **Disaster! What happened next?**

4. At Beijing in 2008 Liu Chang, reigning 110m hurdles champion from 2004, false-started in front of his home fans, injured himself and had to drop out of the race. **Disaster! What happened in 2012?**

5. Guillaume Coekelburg (France) was ahead in the 1908 100 km cycle race when **Disaster!** A judge stepped into his path and made him crash. A few days later, Coekelburg was in the 5000 m race when ... **Double disaster! What happened this time?**

6. In 1988, Greg Louganis (USA) was trying to win the springboard diving event for the second time. He leapt up in the air and ... **Disaster! What happened next?**

7. Jules Noel, of France, was competing in the 1932 discus final. Winding himself up, he launched the furthest throw of the competition. **Disaster! It wasn't allowed! Why not?**

8. Jindrich Suoboda was raring to play for Czechoslovakia against East Germany in the 1980 Olympic football final. But ... **Disaster! He was only named as substitute. What happened next?**

9. In the 1924 rapid-fire pistol shooting, Bailey of USA was shooting in a tie-break for the gold medal. He had to fire six shots in ten seconds. The clock started, and ... **Disaster! Bailey's gun jammed. What happened next?**

10. Sue Platt of Great Britain watched as her third round throw in the 1960 javelin competition soared away to land in the silver medal position. Then ... **Disaster! What happened next?**

11. In 2004 Allen Johnson of the USA got off to a bad start in his 110m hurdles race. After jumping the hurdle 1 ... **Disaster! Accident-prone Allen knocked over hurdles 2, 3, 4 and 5. What happened next?**

12. Competing in the 2004 men's pole vault, Feiliang Liu of China ran up to the bar, thrust his pole into the black hole, soared into the air and ... **Disaster! What happened next?**

13. Alex Partridge was looking forward to competing in the 2004 men's fours rowing event along with colleagues Matthew Pinsent, James Cracknell and Steve Williams when ... **Disaster! He suffered a collapsed lung in training and had to drop out. What happened next?**

Answers:
1. Carjaval lost all his money in a card game and had to hitchhike the rest of the way, just managing to arrive in time for the start. He was still wearing heavy shoes, long trousers and a beret! Somebody cut the legs off his trousers to turn them into shorts, and away Felix went. He managed to come fourth!
2. Vinci lost the extra 200 grams by having a very short haircut – and went on to win the gold medal.
3. Rasmuson fell over a potted plant at the side of the track! Masala overtook him and won the gold medal by just 13 points.
4. Cheesed-off Chang injured himself hitting the first hurdle and collapsed.
5. Another judge stepped in front of Coekelburg and he crashed again!
6. Louganis hit his head on the diving board. But Louganis was a tough nut. He completed the rest of his dives – and won the gold medal!
7. Because all the judges had been watching the pole

vault! They gave Noel another throw, but it was nothing like as good as his other one and he came fourth instead of first. Definitely hell for Noel!

8. Suoboda came on with 19 minutes to go and scored the only goal of the game

9. Bailey calmly unloaded the dud cartridge and fired off five perfect shots in the time he had left. His opponent missed two of his six, and Bailey won the gold.

10. Sue Platt jumped for joy – and stepped over the foul line by mistake! The throw was disallowed and she couldn't manage another one as good. She came fourth, missing out on the medals.

11. Bad turned to worse. Jittery Johnson cleared hurdles 6, 7 and 8 but then tripped over hurdle 9, stumbling so badly that he ended up diving *through* the final hurdle!

12. Unfortunately, Liu didnt soar high enough and went beneath the bar. Even more unfortunately, he didn't soar straight enough. He also missed the landing pit and came down on the grass at the side. You could say he came down to earth with a bump!

13. Alex Partridge's place in the boat was taken by another rower, Ed Coode – and the changed four went on to win the gold medal by just a few centimetres in a thrilling race. But although Alex wasn't there, he hadn't been forgotten. The team had written his name on the front of their boat so that he would be the first man over the line!

Beating the odds

Here are two Olympians who didn't simply have to cope with disastrous situations during their event but throughout their lives.

Hot-shot Karoly

Karoly Takacs of Hungary was a star rapid-fire pistol shooter. Put a pistol in Karoly's steady right hand and you could guarantee he'd hit the target. Then, in 1938, he was involved in a terrible accident. A grenade exploded and his right hand was damaged beyond repair. Karoly would never be able to hold a pistol in it again. So what did tenacious Takacs do? In secret, he began teaching himself to shoot with his left hand. It took ten years, but he did it. In the 1948 London Games, incredible Karoly fired his way to the gold medal.

Stupendous Steve

Do you have trouble reading and writing? Or suffer from an unpleasant illness? Then let Steve Redgrave be your inspiration and you could become a future Olympic medal-winner!

Steve has always been dyslexic. At school he had loads of trouble with his lessons. He didn't get bullied, though, maybe because he was already well on the way to his eventual height of 1.96 m! What's more, in a way English led to him becoming a champion. It was Steve's English teacher who first encouraged him try rowing ... and you could say that young Redgrave took to the sport like a duck to water!

He won his first Olympic gold at Los Angeles in 1984, in the coxed fours event. Seoul in 1988 saw him take another gold, this time in the coxless pairs. Four years on, super Steve won his third gold, again in the coxless pairs. Come 1996 in Atlanta it's the same event again ... and the same result: gold medal number four!

One year later, in 1997, Redgrave got a different kind of result: from a medical test. He was suffering from diabetes, a dangerous condition in which your body doesn't burn up the sugar inside you. Steve began to take his medicine – six injections in the stomach every day! ... and carried on rowing towards Sydney 2000. There he became the greatest British Olympian at that time by winning a fifth gold medal in the coxless fours.

Only now did rower Redgrave retire. After years of non-stop training his doctor told him that he shouldn't just stop doing athletic things but wind down gradually. Steve started his gentle wind-down by running a marathon!

In 2001 Redgrave became Sir Steve in recognition of his achievements. Yes, everybody was agreed that he was the most oarsome Olympian ever!

His Royal Hoy-ness

Steve Redgrave's record British haul of five gold medals lasted until London 2012. There, in the velodrome, super cyclist Chris Hoy powered his way to two more gold medals to add to his one from Athens 2004 and three from Beijing 2008 to give him a sensational six in total. And yet none of his perfect pedalling might have happened if a short-trousered Chris Hoy hadn't been inspired by – what?

(a) a record

(b) a TV programme

(c) a film

Answer (c). It was the film E.T. about a little extra-terrestrial (ie alien) whose departing spaceship accidentally leaves him behind. When the six-year-old Hoy saw the youngsters who meet and help E.T. whizzing around on BMX bikes (and even flying in one scene!), he pestered his mum and dad to buy him a BMX bike too. By the time he was 14, Chris Hoy was ranked the 9th best BMX rider in the world!

BMX biking wasn't an Olympic sport then, so Hoy switched to the track cycling career which ended so brilliantly in 2012. And there in the crowd were the people who bought him that first bike: his proud parents. Mr Hoy waved a home-made placard reading "The Real McHoy"! As for Mrs Hoy – what was she doing?

(a) watching and screaming

(b) hiding her eyes and quivering

Woe is me!

It's obvious what you do when you become a champion. You shout with joy, you laugh, you run a lap of honour.

But what about when you lose?

What do *you* do when things don't go right – for instance, when you're expecting to win the sack race but end up landing on your nose six times and finishing second from last? Do you jump up and down (which is what you should have been doing anyway!) or scream and shout? Do you go home and sulk? Knock the stuffing out of your teddy bear? Teach the parrot rude words?

In 2004, British swimmer Katy Sexton found a wonderful excuse for her poor performances. She found a doctor who announced that she was suffering from 'Unexplained Underperformance Syndrome'. In other words, "Yep, you did badly, but it wasn't your fault!"

141

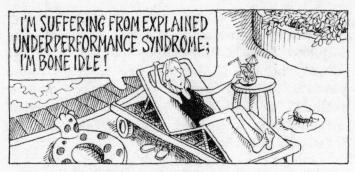

Other Olympic failures have done some far more peculiar things, however...

Short back and sides

● In 1964 Elvira Ozolina (Soviet Union) failed to win the javelin title. She was so disgusted with herself that she marched straight into a hairdressers and had her head shaved.

● Maybe she'd watched the Japanese wrestling team in 1960. After a collection of poor performances they *all* went and had their heads shaved!

Ending it all

● Another Japanese tragically went further. In 1964, with the Games being held in Tokyo, Kokichi

Tsuburaya felt that he'd let his whole country down by only coming third in the marathon (particularly as he'd been overtaken in the stadium itself). He felt his only way of redeeming himself was to win the marathon at the next Games in 1968. When he injured himself and realized he wouldn't be able to take part, he committed suicide.

● Another case of suicide also involved a marathon runner. Ens Fast (Sweden) ran in the 1900 marathon in Paris. This race was run over a very complicated route, and Ens got lost. So, what do you do when you get lost? You ask a policeman to tell you the way. Just what Ens did – only to be told the wrong way! Enough to make anybody suicidal, you might think ... except that it wasn't Ens Fast who killed himself. It was the policeman. Afterwards he was teased about this incident so much that he shot himself. Remember this tragic story next time you're tempted to tease somebody...

Ahoy there!
But, for a really spectacular exhibition of the miseries, there's been little to beat what the British yachtsmen Alan Warren and David Hunt did in 1976.

After their yacht broke down for the third time they set fire to it – then sat in a dinghy to watch it burn! Only when it finally sank to the bottom of Lake Ontario were they satisfied. (I bet they were muttering about 'flaming Olympics', too.)

Flare-ups: flaming Olympic disputes
In the ancient Games the winner of an event got the

olive wreath and the title of champion. But what did those who came second and third get?

a) Nothing.

b) A handshake from the chief judge.

c) A certificate.

d) A picture of an olive wreath.

Answer: a) Nothing. Only winners got prizes in the ancient Games.

In spite of the athletes' oath, in the Olympics, winning has usually been all-important. That means that in any close contest there'll be arguments about who's actually won. And in the Olympics there have been plenty of arguments!

Usually, the judges are in the middle of things. After all, settling arguments is what they're there for. But sometimes they're the cause of the argument...

● In the 1920 football final, Belgium were beating Czechoslovakia 2-0 when the Czechs walked off because they thought the referee was being unfair.

● In the 1972 basketball final, the USA were beating Russia by one point with one second to go

144

when the judges decided that the clock was wrong. They had it put back by two seconds ... giving Russia enough time to score the winning basket and stop USA winning the basketball gold for the eighth time in sucession.

● The judges decided that John Devitt (Australia) had just beaten Lance Larson (USA) in the 1960 100 m freestyle swimming. The result had to stand – even though the electronic timing devices made Larson 0.1 seconds faster! (After this dispute, electronic times were always used to decide the results of swimming events.)

Silent protests

Sometimes, the best way of protesting is to say nothing – but just get on and win. Here are two who did just that.

● Forrest Smithson was a theology student who, in 1908, objected to the final of the 110 m hurdles being held on a Sunday. His way of protesting was to be pictured with a Bible in his left hand. He won, too, in world-record time!

● A similar case in 1924 was that of the Scottish runner, Eric Liddell, whose story was told in the film *Chariots of Fire*. He wouldn't run in his 100 m heat on a Sunday, full stop. So he ran on another day in the 400 m instead – and won it in an Olympic record time.

Seconds out!

Then there was the case of the silent protest which didn't do any good.

● In 1988, the Korean boxer Byun Jong-II was penalized for butting. After losing his bout he staged a sit-down protest, refusing to leave the ring. He stayed put for 67 minutes (enough time to have fought another 22 rounds), but the judges didn't change their minds.

Some athletes don't make a fuss or protest when things go wrong. When the favourite for the 1996 women's 5,000 m, Sonia Sullivan of Ireland, had to drop out after a nasty bout of diarrhoea before a race, she refused to make excuses. "I'm a person who likes to keep everything inside me," she said!

THE CENTENNIAL QUIZ

Atlanta 1996 saw the modern Olympics celebrate their 100th birthday – and, as ever, there were hundreds of flaming incidents!

So here's a Centennial quiz – kind of. The questions all feature the number 100 ... or just 1 ... or sometimes a pathetic 0!

1. One of the finalists in the 100 m was a grandfather. **True or False?**

2. The winner of the 100 m was Donovan Bailey (Canada) who powered down the track at an average speed of 22.54 miles per hour. One group of competitors in the Olympic swimming pool went even faster, though. **True or False?**

3. Hong Kong won one gold medal in 1996. What was so special about it?
a) It was the first they'd ever won.
b) It was the last they'll ever win.

4. In the 141 lb class of the weightlifting competition, Tony Analou of the Soloman Islands lifted a grand total of 0 lbs, and yet managed to break the Asian record. **True or False?**

5. After the Games were over, $100 would have bought you five official souvenirs at $19.95 each and left you with 25c change. What were they?

a) A replica gold medal.

b) A piece of the athletics track.

c) A ten-minute video of the Olympic flame burning.

6. The USA were the top medal winners with 100 + 1 medals. But if the calculation had been based on the number of medals per citizen, where would they have finished?

a) 10th.

b) 25th.

c) 39th.

7. Beach volleyball was first played as an official sport in 1996. How many Atlanta beaches were available to choose from? Clue: the answer uses only the digits 1 or 0.

8. Shooting star Michael Diamond won gold for Australia in his event. The time difference meant that this took place at 7 am in his home country. The TV cameras were there ... so how many Australians saw Diamond's winning shot as it happened? Same clue again: the answer uses only the digits 1 or 0.

Answers:

1. True. Linford Christie of Great Britain was a grandfather when he lined up for the final. Did that mean his reactions were slow and doddery? Quite the opposite, unfortunately. He was guilty of two false starts and was disqualified!

2. True. Every single high diver. Good or bad, they all hit the water at 31 miles per hour!

3. a) Lee Lai Shan won Hong Kong's first gold for sailboarding. Hong Kong has since become part of China but, as it still competes under its own flag, it needn't be the last!

4. True – and False. A computer error caused every competitor in the event to be credited with breaking the Asian record, even if (like the Soloman Islands) their country wasn't in Asia and if (like the 0 lbs poor Tony Analou scored after failing to lift anything!) their total didn't break the record.

5. b). Amazingly, when the Games ended, the athletics track was torn up and the stadium turned into a baseball ground.

6. c), with one medal per 2.6 million citizens. Bottom would have been India, with just one medal to show for their 936 million citizens. Top place went to the tiny island of Tonga, whose one medal came from just 105,600 citizens.

7. 0! Atlanta is 650 miles from the nearest real beach! Five hundred tonnes of sand were shipped in and two artifical courts made up.

8. 0 again! The TV channel showing the event interrupted it for a commercial break – during which Diamond took his winning shot!

Centennial did you know

The most valuable item of Olympic memorabilia is a piece of paper. It's the letter Baron Pierre de Coubertin wrote to restart the Olympic Games in 1896 and is insured for $100,000.

OH, BLOW! - THE CLOSING CEREMONY

The Olympics open with a great ceremony. They close with one too. So did the ancient Games. In those days the ceremony amounted to:

- Prize-giving of olive wreaths to the champions (but nothing to the runners-up, remember).
- Giving of thanks to Zeus for looking after the Games.
- A winner's banquet, at which the sacrificial oxen were cooked and everybody ate every body.

WELL, AFTER THIS WE WON'T BE DOING ANY SPORT FOR A WHILE!

For the modern Olympics in 1896 things on the final day were pretty much the same, apart from the fact that nobody gave thanks to Zeus and there weren't any oxen to eat and this time the runners-up did get something...

- Champions got a silver medal (not gold), an olive branch and a diploma.
- Runners-up got a copper medal, a laurel branch and a diploma.

In 1928, though, the medal-giving ceremonies and the closing ceremony were separated. Now, medals are awarded to first, second and third soon after the event has finished in ceremonies that close with the national anthem of the winner's country.

Flaming Facts
- Bronze medals for third-placed contestants were awarded for the first time in 1904.
- In the early years, winners of team events (for instance, 4 x 100 m relay in athletics) had to share one medal.
- The victory stand, with its 1 – 2 – 3 positions, was introduced in 1932.

- An Olympic gold medal is only worth about £275. This is because over 90% of it isn't gold at all, but solid silver. There's only 6 grams of gold covering it – but to the winner it's priceless!

Gimme me medal!

You might think that nothing much could go wrong at a medal-giving ceremony. Wrong! There have been some red faces throughout the history of the Games…

What happened next?

1. 1912. Jim Thorpe (USA) stands ready to receive his medal from King Gustav V of Sweden. The King says to Thorpe, "Sir, you are the greatest athlete in the world." Jim Thorpe says…

2. 1924. Harold Abrahams (Britain) hears a rattle at his letterbox. There's a package on the mat. He opens it. Out drops…

3. 1936. Japanese pole vaulters Shuhei Nishida and Sueo Oe finish equal second in the pole vault. They refuse to jump off for second and third places, but there is only one silver medal and one bronze…

4. 1956. Rower Vyacheslav Ivanov (Soviet Union) is so excited about winning his medal he throws it in the air – but fails to catch it…

5. 1964. Abebe Bikila receives his gold medal for winning the Marathon. The Ethiopian flag begins to rise as the band strikes up…

6. 1972. Dave Wottle (USA), who always runs in an old golf cap, receives his medal for the 800 m. The American anthem strikes up, and Wottle turns solemnly towards the flag…

Answers:

1. "Thanks, King!"

2. His 100 m gold medal. There were no presentation ceremonies at the 1924 Games.

3. They took them home to Japan where they asked a jeweller to cut the medals in half, then weld them together so that they both had a medal that was half silver and half bronze!

4. And it plopped into the waters of Lake Wendouree! Ivanov was given another one. (Attention Australian treasure hunters: the original medal has never been found!)

5. And plays the Japanese national anthem! The band didn't know the Ethiopian anthem.

6. But forgets to take his cap off. He appeared on TV later, crying as he apologized to the American public.

The closing ceremony

Here we are then, at the closing ceremony. It's a grand affair, with lots going on. Which of the following *won't* you expect to see?

- Flag bearers of national flags and six team members from each country parading into the stadium.

- All the other competitors coming in together to show that they're united in sport.

- Three national anthems being played – of Greece, of the host country, and of the country to be hosts next time.

- A closing speech being made (of course!).
- The mayor of the city hosting the next Games receiving the ceremonial Olympic flag to look after.
- The Olympic flame being extinguished.
- The Olympic flag that has flown throughout the Games being taken down and paraded out of the Stadium.
- A UFO landing in the middle of the arena.

Answer: They all usually happen, except the last one.

But in 1984 in Los Angeles a UFO did land right in the middle of the arena. Out stepped an 'alien'…

Except that – surprise! surprise! – he wasn't a real alien. He was actually a student, specially chosen for what the organizers thought were his alien looks: he was 7 ft 8 ins (2.44 m) tall! His job was to emphasize what a good thing the Olympic Games had been by saying: "I've come a long way, because I like what I've seen!"

After the games are over...

What do Olympic athletes do when the Games are over? Some, of course, carry on competing. There are National Championships, European Championships, and World Championships in most sports nowadays.

But what about life outside sport? Many competitors go back to their jobs. Some go on to do other things. See how you get on with this final quiz about Olympic competitors and what they got up to after they'd finished competing...

1. The 1900 marathon champion earned so little dough from his victory that he returned to his job working for:
a) A butcher.
b) A baker.
c) A candlestick maker.

2. After locking up his gold medal, the 1920 middleweight boxing champion returned to his job as:
a) A policeman.
b) A bus driver.
c) A road sweeper.

3. After lording it in the pool, the winner of five swimming gold medals in 1924 and 1928 went on to star in lots of films as:
a) Tarzan.
b) Superman.
c) Batman.

4. The prayerful 1924 men's 400 m champion raced off to become:

a) A vicar in London.
b) A monk in Tibet.
c) A missionary in China.

5. The winner of a silver medal for weightlifting in 1948 later tried to cap it all by doing something very unpleasant to James Bond. Was it:
a) Slice him in half with a laser beam.
b) Cut his head off.
c) Tuck him up in bed with a tarantula.

6. The 1960 decathlon gold medallist later became a powerful performer as:
a) An actor.
b) A pop singer.
c) A bodyguard.

7. After being 'throne' by her horse, a member of a 1976 equestrian team went home and continued to be:
a) A princess
b) The daughter of somebody very famous
c) The mother of a future gold medallist

Answers:
1. b) Michel Theato (France) worked as a baker's roundsman.

YOU CAN'T LOAF AROUND!

158

2. a) Harry Mallin (Britain) was a policeman.

3. a) Johnny Weismuller (USA) made a highly successful switch from swimming between ropes to swinging from them!

4. c) After his famous stand against running on a Sunday, Eric Liddell (Britain) went on to be a missionary.

5. b) Harold Sakata (USA) later played the meanie 'Oddjob' in the James Bond film *Goldfinger* in which he tried to cut the hero's head off with his steel-edged bowler hat.

6. a) and **c)** Rafer Johnson became an actor (appearing with Elvis Presley in one film – but

with Elvis doing the singing) and then bodyguard
to Senator Robert Kennedy.

7. All three! Apart from continuing to be a
princess and the somebody famous' daughter,
Princess Anne was also the mother of Zara
Phillips, a member of Britain's 2012 winning
equestrian team – where the proud mother
performed the medal-giving ceremony!

Last, but not least, there's the world-famous Briton
who won a bronze in the heavyweight wrestling.
Everybody knew what he looked like, but hardly
anybody knew that his name was Ken Richmond.

Even you probably know what he looks like, but
I bet you don't know his name is Ken Richmond
either.

Why? Because he's the strongman who whacks
the gong at the start of the old films on TV.

Beat that if you can!

FLAMING OLYMPICS 2016

Will there be any flaming stories from Rio de Janeiro to go into the next edition of this book? Of course! There's never been an Olympics Games yet that hasn't produced its own collection of champs and chumps, disputes and disasters.

Flaming Fact

In 1896, the first Modern Olympics champion was USA triple-jumper James Connolly with a winning jump of 13.71m. In 2016 that won't be good enough to qualify for the women's triple-jump final – 14.20m is required – let alone the men's, which requires a mighty 16.90m!

The events in 2016 will be spread across four 'zones' of the city: Deodoro in the north, Barra in the south, and – the two best known by far – Maracanã and Copacabana in the east.

The opening and closing ceremonies will be held in the magnificent Maracanã Stadium. Don't think that it's being built specially for the Olympics, though. The stadium was constructed in 1950 when the football World Cup was held in Brazil. A world-record crowd of 200,000 packed into the stadium for the final match to see the host country lose to deadly rivals Uruguay.

The Maracanã has been updated lots of times since 1950, of course, as you'll see when it also stages the final of the 2016 Olympic football tournament. But don't expect the crowd to be anything like as big. The stadium is now all-seater and can take a maximum crowd of about 75,000.

Flaming Fact
The name Maracanã comes from an old word for a type of parrot which lived in the area.
Maybe that's why fans in the Maracanã make so much noise!

Collosal Copacabana
Copacabana is famous for its beach – all 4km of it! It's so big that every New Year's Eve about 2 million people squeeze on to it to watch fireworks at midnight. The sand is so soft that, for once, there'll be no need to find some good enough for beach volleyball; it's where the game began, after all!

The waves that come cascading on to the shore are also world famous, so Copacabana is where the sailing and water sports events will be held too. Sounds great? It will be so long as the competitors don't fall in. Tests have shown that Rio's sewage system isn't yet as good as it could be and that the sea off the beach contains rather more bugs than you'd want. A competitor who swallows too much of it could spend a lot of time in the loo afterwards!

Finally, here's a short quiz on a few more things to look out for in 2016 ...

A. The 100 m and 200 m champion, Usain Bolt of Jamaica, will be hoping to retain the titles he won in Beijing 2008 and London 2012. When he won gold in the Beijing 100 m, how did he finish the race?
a) looking at the stadium's TV screen.
b) going as fast as the car he won as a prize.
c) with one of his laces undone.

B. Another Jamaican sprinter who hopes to go to Rio and defend the titles she won in Beijing and London is the reigning women's 100 m champion Shelly-Ann Fraser-Pryce. She said her wins might all be down to her mum. Why?
a) for being a good runner herself.
b) for feeding her good Jamaican food.
c) for mending her running shorts.

C. For Rio 2016 all the stadium announcers will speak in Portuguese. True or False?

D. If the 2016 Olympics follow the same pattern as 2012 then a lot of baby girls will be named Jessica (after Ennis). Following Beijing in 2008, though, a lot of new-born babies were named – what?
a) Olympics.
b) Torch.
c) Goldie.

Answers
A – c). In spite of this, bulleting Bolt still broke the world record! However, If you picked a), you weren't far wrong. He admitted doing this in the 200 m final and thinking to himself, "this guy is fast!" No wonder he ended the Games with the nickname 'Lightning Bolt'!

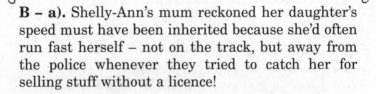

Flaming Fact
Unfortunately, Usain Bolt's driving wasn't as hot as his running. He was given a car for winning the 2008 Olympic 100 metres – and crashed it!

B – a). Shelly-Ann's mum reckoned her daughter's speed must have been inherited because she'd often run fast herself – not on the track, but away from the police whenever they tried to catch her for selling stuff without a licence!

C – False. The official languages of the Olympic Movement are French and English, so stadium announcements – plus official posters and even the temporary street signs – will be in both languages.

D – a). In China, before the 2008 Games even began, over 4,000 children had been named Aoyun, which means "Olympics". Nine out of ten of them were boys.

One thing's certain, though. "Olympic Torch Scroggins" may not feature in the newspaper headlines, but in Rio de Janeiro in 2016 there'll be loads of other names that hit the headlines. Some will be the names of wonderful winners. Others will be those of lousy losers. But that's the way it's always been.

It's what makes the Olympics so much flaming fun!

LONDON 2012 REMEMBERED

It seems like only yesterday that the Olympic Games were held in London – but it was all of four years ago!

Were you there in London, or did you watch the action on TV? How many different sports did you follow? Perhaps you enjoyed the awesome athletics and raved about the rowing. Or celebrated the cyling or gibbered joyfully over the gymnastics. Maybe you visited the volleyball or took in the taekwondo? Could be you simply settled for fuming at Team GB's failure in the football ...

Whatever your memories of London 2012, in this section you'll get the chance to relive them – and discover some fascinatingly flaming facts that you may have missed!

Then and now
London is the only city in the world that has hosted the Summer Games three times. Apart from 2012, the Games had previously been held in London in 1948 – and, before that, way back in 1908.

Try this quiz to discover what had changed over the years. What would a 10-year-old spectator at the 1908 Games have noticed when the Olympics came back to London for a second time in 1948, or during that wonderful third visit in 2012 (apart from the fact they were 114 years old themselves!)?

For each of these London Olympics facts, decide whether it applies to 1908, 1948 or 2012. We'll start with some general facts.

1. The Olympic Torch arrived from Greece and was carried by a relay of 8000 torch-bearers on a journey round the United Kingdom. **1908**, **1948** or **2012**?

2. The main events took place in 'The Great Stadium'. **1908**, **1948** or **2012**?

3. The competitors slept in private houses or army barracks. **1908**, **1948** or **2012**?

4. A programme cost 2½p and the top price for a ticket to watch the opening ceremony was over £2000. **1908**, **1948** or **2012**?

5. One of the events was a competition for artists. **1908**, **1948** or **2012**?

6. Now for some facts about sports. In the Olympic tennis events, women players wore skirts. **1908**, **1948** or **2012**?

7. Polo featured as a sport. **1908**, **1948** or **2012**?

8. There were swimming events which took place in the open air. **1908**, **1948** or **2012**?

9. Sand played an important part in the Games. **1908**, **1948** or **2012**?

10. The cycling events featured a bicycle made for two. **1908**, **1948** or **2012**?

Answers
1. 2012. The Olympic Torch arrived on 18th May and was carried on a 70-day journey to towns and cities throughout England, Scotland, Wales and Northern Ireland. In 1908 there was no relay at all, because the tradition hadn't yet begun. In 1948 the relay was a smaller affair, taking only 12 days and being carried by just over 1400 torchbearers.

2. 1908. The Great Stadium was built at a place

called the White City, in London. Afterwards it was mainly used for greyhound racing before being knocked down in 1985. It cost £60,000 to build. The 1948 stadium cost nothing – kind of. It was the old Wembley Stadium, the one knocked down in 2003 to make way the new stadium that's there now. As for the 2012 Olympic Stadium ... get your calculators out ... that cost £9,345,000,000 (£9.345 billion). In other words, for the cost of the 2012 stadium you could have built 155,750 Great Stadiums in 1908!

3. 1948. The 1948 Games were the first to take place after World War II, and there wasn't the money or materials for special accommodation for athletes. Some lived with families, but most men were put up in army camps. The women were a little bit better off. They stayed in college dormitories. Male or female, though, one report said that athletes were lucky if they had a half share of a locker and a mirror! In 2012 the athletes lived in a special village and got through over a quarter of a million loaves of bread! And in 1908? Simple – competitors were expected to find their own place to live. When they arrived in London they were all given a handy guide to hotels or guesthouses!

4. 1908 ... and 2012. The price of a summary programme in 1908 was just 2½p – which is worth about £2.20 now. In 1948 the price of a programme and visitors' guide had gone up to 12½p (about £3.60 now). There were also programmes for

169

different events, which cost 5p (about £1.40 now). In 2012 a single-day programme cost £5 – and a top price ticket for the opening ceremony an amazing £2012!

5. 1948. The competition was for works of art that had been inspired by sport, with medals to be won in five 'events': writing, painting, music, sculpture and building. It should have started in 1908 but there wasn't enough time for entries to be completed. 1948 saw the last arts competition – not because of a lack of interest but because the Olympics were supposed to be for amateurs and artists were people who got paid for their work. The arts competitions were turned into 'cultural programmes' instead, with no winners or losers. In 2012 there was a London 2012 Festival at which musicians, dancers, sculptors, film-makers and the like got the chance to show off but not win any medals.

6. 1908 and 2012. The difference is that in 2012 women's skirts were short; in 1908 they were down to the ground. In 1948, though, women tennis players wore no skirts at all – not because they'd left them off, but because tennis didn't feature in the 1948 Olympics.

7. 1908, 1948 and 2012 – but not always the same kind of polo! Water polo was included each time, but 1908 also featured the kind of polo that involves players charging about on horses. By 1948 the organizers had said *neigh more!*, and the event had been dropped.

8. 1908 and 2012. In 1908 every swimming event took place in the open air. That's because the 100 m swimming pool was slap-bang in the middle of "The Great Stadium" with the athletics track outside it! By 1948 all the swimming events had moved indoors. By 2012 they were swimming outdoors again. A 10 km swimming 'marathon' was started in 2008, with both men's and women's events.

9. 1908, 1948 and 2012. In 1908 and 1948 sand was the stuff that long-jumpers, triple-jumpers, high-jumpers and pole-vaulters would land in. In 2012 that was only true for long-jumpers and triple-jumpers. By then the high-jumpers and pole-vaulters were going so high that sand wasn't good enough to land in; they needed lots of foam-filled stuff. This loss of sand was more than made up for by the recent introduction of beach volleyball, which featured again in 2012 – they needed tonnes of it!

10. 1908 and 1948 both had tandem events in the

cycling. There was no such event in 2012 as it was punctured years ago.

Awesome arenas

Winning the contest to become the Olympic Games' host city takes a lot effort – but it takes even more effort after you have won it! That's why the host city is selected seven years in advance: it gives the organizers time to sort everything out.

Top of the list, of course, is building or preparing the venues for the different sporting events. To do this, there are always three possible choices:

a) use an existing venue.

b) change an existing venue to make it suitable.

c) build a new venue from scratch.

For example, if your school won the right to host a mini-Olympics you might decide to:

a) use your existing school field for the football, athletics and archery (but not at the same time!).

b) change your school hall by raising the ceiling up higher so as to make it suitable for badminton and gymnastics.

c) build a temporary new pool in the playground for the swimming and diving events.

I DON'T KNOW WHAT BIRDS THEY ARE, BUT THEY'RE FAST!

That's just how it was for the venues used in London 2012. Some were suitable as they were, some had to be adapted and some were completely new. Here are seven of the best known. Match them to the sports they hosted:

A. Horse Guards Parade
B. Hyde Park
C. Lords Cricket Ground
D. The O2 Arena
E. Wembley Stadium
F. Wimbledon
G. Olympic Park

1. Gymnastics and Basketball

2. Football

3. Athletics

4. Triathlon

5. Archery

6. Beach Volleyball

7. Tennis

Answers:

A-6: Needless to say, they had to bring in a beach from somewhere. It came from the Godstone sand pits in Surrey – about 2500 tonnes of it! After the Games were over, the sand was recycled to create new beach volleyball courts around London.

B-4: The swimming part of the Triathlon took place in the Serpentine lake in Hyde Park. The 10 km open-water swimming event was also held there.

C-5: Where no archer wanted to score a duck! (And none did.)

D-1: But obviously not at the same time! What happened was a bit like the end of one of your gym lessons at school. Once all the vaulting and somersaulting was over, the equipment and mats were cleared away and the O2 was converted into a basketball arena.

E-2: The final was, anyway. Preliminary matches were held at famous football grounds around Britain.

F-7: Wimbledon? Tennis? Now there's a surprise!

G-3: The Olympic Park was the centrepiece of the Games, with different buildings for different events. The Velodrome saw the cycling and the Aquatics Centre the swimming. The athletics events took place (like the opening and closing ceremonies) in the Olympic Stadium.

Flaming Fact

Not only do you have to have the right type of ball for beach volleyball, you have to have the right type of sand as well. Check out your nearest beach to see if it fits the Olympic rules, which say the sand must be:

- white, to reflect heat and not burn skin
- firm enough to help players jump
- soft enough for them to land in
- made up of equally-sized, non-scratchy grains

Once upon a time: awesome arena facts

Whether they were ready to go, had to be adapted or were completely new, each of those London 2012 arenas had one thing in common: an entertaining history. They'd all been built on land that had previously been used for something completely different. Use these historical facts to tantalise your teachers and fool your friends!

Henry's horses

King Henry VIII wasn't only interested in marrying wives and chopping their heads off. He enjoyed sports as well. One of his favourite sports was jousting – a contest in which two riders with very long poles charged at each other from opposite directions.

That's what the big flat area called Horse Guards Parade was once used for: it was Henry VIII's jousting arena.

Henry's hunts

Another sport Henry VIII enjoyed was hunting (for wives, of course, but also for deer). That's where Hyde Park comes into the picture. Henry acquired it from the church in 1536 and used it as a place to raise deer – then, when they were fully grown, to chase after them!

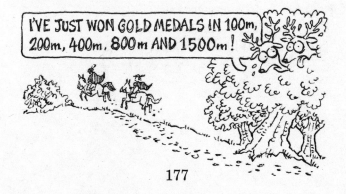

It's not cricket!

Archery was able to be held at the Lord's cricket ground because cricket wasn't in the Olympics. But if history had been different we could have seen an entirely different event to both of them taking place there. The current Lord's ground is a couple of hundred metres down the road from where it was in 1813. Why did it move? Because otherwise the newly-built Regents Canal would have run straight through the outfield. Yes, Lord's could have been where the rowing events were held!

Oh two pooh

Basketball and gymnastics took place in the O2 Arena as it is now called. Before that it was known as the Millennium Dome, home to an exhibition that was set up in the year 2000. But that was built on top of land that had been used as a dumping ground for sludge from a gasworks.

Watkin's Wembley wobbler

The Olympic football final, and some of the other matches, took place at England's top football ground, Wembley Stadium, which only opened in 2007. What was there before that? The first Wembley Stadium, the place where England won the football world cup in 1966. That ground was built in 1923. And what was there before that? Watkin's Tower, that's what.

Sir Edward Watkin was a dreamer who wanted to build a rival to the Eiffel Tower, in Paris. Work on "The Great Tower of London" as it was called, began in 1892. It soon ran in to trouble. After four years the tower's ironwork had reached only 50 metres of its intended 358 metres. Worse, it was getting lower by the day – because it had started sinking! In the end the project was scrapped and the little that had been built was blown up.

New balls, please!

Tennis is the sport for which Wimbledon is world-famous, of course. But did you know that the full name of the club which owns the courts is The All England Lawn Tennis and Croquet Club? It's had that name since 1877, the year when the first Wimbledon tennis tournament was held.

Before that, from its beginnings in 1868, it was just the All England Croquet Club – that is, a club devoted to the game which involves knocking coloured balls through hoops. Croquet was incredibly popular in those days, which is why the first Olympic games in 1896 had croquet as one of its sports. After all, it's a game played by royalty. The Queen of Hearts plays it in the famous book *Alice in Wonderland* ... using flamingos for mallets and live hedgehogs for balls!

Olympic Park: what a lot of rubbish!
Athletics, swimming, cycling, hockey and a variety of other sports took place at the brand-new Olympic Park. What was there before? Lots of things!
• Skeletons which were about 2,000 years old.
• Newts and toads which (unlike the skeletons) were alive and kicking. They were all caught and transferred to ponds built especially for them.
• Loads and loads of rubbish, especially rubbish made out of plastic.

Nobody could complain about the plastic rubbish, though. That's because, in the 1800s, the whole area used to be full of factories – one of which played a vital part in the invention of … you've guessed it, plastic!

The best of British
At London 2012 Team GB, as the British squad were known, made the most of 'playing at home' by winning gold medals in no fewer than 29 events. Here's a complete timetable of those heroic happenings – together with a few fascinating facts!

1st August 2012
• In the road cycling, and just a few days after winning the Tour de France, Bradley Wiggins took gold in the individual time trial. It brought his Olympic medal total to a super seven – joint highest for a British athlete with fellow cyclist Chris Hoy.
• Rowers Helen Glover and Heather Stanning won the women's pairs. But if it hadn't been for some quick thinking, Glover may not have made the team. She was a little bit under the minimum height set for

candidates for top training – so when it came to being measured, she stood on tip-toe!

2nd August 2012

• Philip Hindes, Jason Kenny and Chris Hoy won the cycling team sprint.

• Canoeists Etienne Stott and Tim Baillie won the C2 slalom event. The day after, Stott got a big shock. He was walking down the street and somebody recognized him. It had never happened before!

• In the double trap shooting, Peter Wilson took gold – and it still wasn't enough to get him recognized! He was travelling on the tube a week later and sitting beside two boys who were talking about the Olympics. They only realized who Wilson was when he offered them a close-up look at the gold medal he had in his jacket pocket!

3rd August 2012

• Another rowing gold, this time for Katherine Grainger and Anna Watkins in the double sculls. For Grainger it was fourth time lucky – she'd won silver medals at each of the three previous Olympics.

• In the cycling team pursuit semi-final, Ed Clancy, Steven Burke, Peter Kennaugh and Geraint Thomas set a new world record time – only to see it broken in the final. Who by? Themselves, as they powered their way to the gold medal!

• The women's keirin cycling event was won by Victoria Pendleton. She retired after London 2012, saying that she planned to continue training ... in something completely different: cake decorating!

4th August 2012

This was a Saturday, and such a successful one that it has gone down in British Olympic history as "Super Saturday"...

• It began with yet another rowing gold as Andrew Triggs Hodge, Tom James, Peter Reed and Alex Gregory won the men's four event.

• Katherine Copeland and Sophie Hosking followed it up by taking gold in the women's lightweight double sculls. What did the delighted Copeland shout to her partner as they crossed the line? "We've won gold?" No – "We're going to be on a stamp!" The Royal Mail were honouring all the winning Olympians by bringing out special stamps with their pictures on them, and Copeland was really excited at the thought of being stuck on an envelope and not in a boat.

• Back on the cycling track Laura Trott, Dani King and Joanna Rowsell won the women's team pursuit, making it a doubly special day for racing Rowsell. She suffers from a condition called alopecia – losing your hair at an early age – and as 4th August was also International Alopecia Day it meant that seeing her receive a gold medal showed other sufferers that they could still do great things, hair or not.
• Into the Olympic Stadium now, for some amazing athletics. Jessica Ennis, who had been 'The Face of the Games' with her picture seeming to be on almost

every London 2012 poster, finished off two days of action to clinch victory in the heptathlon.

• Then long-jumper Greg Rutherford leapt to a gold medal – which he said afterwards was a reward for all the support he'd had from his watching Mum and Dad.

• Finally, Mo Farah finished off Super Saturday with a scorching win in the 10,000 m. At the end he celebrated by performing his 'mobot' action, joining his hands on the top of his head to form the letter 'M' for 'Mo'.

5th August 2012
• Next day, on the centre court at Wimbledon, Andy Murray netted the men's singles tennis title. Afterwards he said that he'd watched the athletics the previous evening and that had inspired him.

• Ben Ainslie won his fourth successive sailing gold medal in the 'Finn' class, thanks to Rita. Was Rita his first sailing instructor? His wife? No, Rita was his boat!

6th August 2012

• The cycling individual sprint event was won by Jason Kenny – much to his relief. Only one sprinter was allowed per country and Kenny had been chosen ahead of reigning champion Chris Hoy. That's why at the starting line jittery Jason had told himself: "I'd better not mess this one up!"

• Over in the show-jumping arena, British riders Nick Skelton, Scott Brash, Peter Charles and Ben Maher won the team show-jumping gold. Skelton was the veteran of the group. Aged 54 he'd been riding since he was 18 months old – not counting a spell off after injuring himself in 2000. He'd broken his neck!

7th August 2012

• Charlotte Dujardin, Carl Hester and Laura Bechtolsheimer then won Britain's first-ever medal in equestrian dressage, winning the event riding their horses Valegro, Uthopia and … er, Alf.

• In another nail-biting moment, Alistair Brownlee became Team GB's first triathlon champion. On the podium with him was his brother Johnny, who won the bronze medal.

• Back in the velodrome, Laura Trott did better than 'trot round' in the omnium event – she sped round at record speed to win another gold. Next day her picture was in all the papers. Cycling? No, sharing a kiss with boyfriend and fellow cycling gold-medallist Jason Kenny!

•Best of all, Chris Hoy won his sixth gold medal in cycling's keirin event to beat Steve Redgrave's five golds and become Britains's most succesful Olympian ever. So pleased was he about this that Heroic Hoy spent the whole of the victory ceremony in tears!

9th August 2012

• Charlotte Dujardin added to her team dressage gold by winning the individual gold medal as well. She then celebrated as she had the first time, with a river boat trip on the Thames.

• With the arrival of women's boxing at the Olympics, Nicola Adams went down in history as Britain's first gold medallist in the sport by winning the flyweight division. As soon as the fight was over, she just couldn't wait to show it to Dexter. Her boyfriend? No – her puppy dog, who'd been in kennels since London 2012 began!

• Jade Jones' gold in the taekwondo under 57 kg class produced yet another first-time winner for Team GB. Jade's win impressed girls who wanted to take after her (and dazzled some lads so much they sent texts asking her to marry them!).

11th August 2012

• Back out on the water, Ed McKeever won the K1 200 m canoe sprint. Not long after, 'appy Ed got married (not to Jade Jones!). Did all the guests queue up for a look at his gold medal? No, he'd deliberately left it at home to ensure that his bride would be the centre of attention.

• Luke Campbell, from Hull, won the bantamweight boxing title. To mark the occasion the Hull Daily Mail printed a special souvenir edition.

• On the final day of the athletics, 10,000 m champion Mo Farah completed a fantastic double by winning the 5,000 m as well. And, just as they had before, his wife Tania and stepdaughter Rhianna joined him on the track to celebrate.

12th August 2012

• Last, but not least, on the final day of the London 2012 Olympics, Anthony Joshua won gold in boxing's super-heavyweight division – then hurried back home to show his medal to his cousin, Benga, who'd encouraged him to take up boxing in the first place. Benga had even given him a pair of shorts and loaned him £25 to buy some boots!

The best-ever Olympic marathon route quiz

Olympic marathons usually start and end in a stadium but take to the roads in between. Judging from the story of Pheidippedes, it didn't sound as though he stopped to admire the scenery during his original run from Marathon to Athens. The runners in 2012 didn't have time to stop either – which was a shame for them because the marathon route went past famous London landmarks that were not only good to look at, but which were dripping with all sorts of flaming historical details. You can admire them, though, with the help of this quiz. Match these ten marathon route landmarks with the correct detail; but be warned – some of them aren't very nice!

1. Admiralty Arch	**A**. An old lady
2. Nelson's Column	**B**. Gruesome executions
3. St Paul's Cathedral	**C**. A flaming pot!
4. The Bank of England	**D**. A ghostly monk
5. St Clement's Church	**E**. A baby's bottle
6. The Tower of London	**F**. A flaming plot!
7. Monument	**G**. War-time survivor
8. Cleopatra's Needle	**H**. Wellington's nose
9. The Houses of Parliament	**I**. A drowned saint
10. Buckingham Palace	**J**. A shot sailor

Answers

1–H: Every runner would have been hoping to get their nose in front at the finishing line, so passing through Admiralty Arch should have inspired them. Sticking out from the inside of one arch is a replica of a human nose. It's reputed to be there in honour of the famous and big-nosed general the Duke of Wellington. Soldiers riding through the arch will still rub the hooter for good luck, but any runner who'd wanted to do the same would have had to jump a bit – Wellington's Nose is over 2 metres off the ground!

2–J: Nelson's Column should have reminded the

runners that they'd got a battle ahead of them. It's a memorial to Admiral Horatio Nelson who was shot and killed at the Battle of Trafalgar in 1805. The column is 51.59 metres tall, from its base to the top of Nelson's hat – about a metre less than the height of the Olympic Stadium.

3–G: Every marathon runner's hope is that they'll at least survive to the end of the race. The sight of St Paul's Cathedral should have spurred them on. In 1940, during the Second World War, much of London was flattened by bombs – but the cathedral miraculously survived.

4–A: The Bank of England is on Threadneedle Street in London. It's been in business since 1694, which is why its nickname is 'The Old Lady of Threadneedle Street.' The marathon medal winners couldn't have found a much safer place to deposit their precious prizes after the race. Opening the bank's vaults needs three keys, each of which is about a metre long!

5–I: Marathon running is thirsty work, so St Clement's Church was an appropriate place to have on the route. For one thing it's said to be the church referred to in the famous playground rhyme 'Oranges and Lemons' (*say the bells of St Clements*). And, for another, St Clement himself knew all about being 'in the drink'. He's the patron saint of sailors – because he was murdered for his Christian beliefs by being tied to an anchor and chucked into the sea!

6–B: The runners would have been able to see the Tower of London but the route didn't take them very close too it. In 1536, King Henry VIII's wife Anne Boleyn would have been happy not to have gone very close to it too. It's where she had her head chopped off!

7–C: By this stage in the race the runners would have been really warmed up – making The Monument a perfect landmark on the route because it commemorates the Great Fire of London in 1666. The column measures 203 feet (61 metres, 87 centimetres) from top to bottom: the exact distance from its base to nearby Pudding Lane, where the fire broke out in a baker's shop. At the top of the column sits a flaming copper urn as a reminder of what happened.

8–E: As they reached Cleopatra's Needle, the runners would not have wanted to be suffering from a 'stitch'! Located on the Thames Embankment, this famous landmark was erected in 1878. Buried beneath it is a time capsule from that year containing such things as toys, a set of coins, a portrait of Queen Victoria – and a baby's bottle.

9–F: In 1605, Guy Fawkes and a group of other plotters were caught getting ready to blow up the Houses of Parliament. The 2012 marathon runners went round London, and poor old Guy did the same in a way. After being hanged his body was chopped up and the various bits sent to different places in the city to be put on show!

10–D: The runners would have known that the finishing line was close when they spotted Buckingham Palace. Hopefully, they didn't spot anything else. Buckingham Palace stands on the site of what was once a priory and it's said that a ghostly, chain-draped monk in a brown habit sometimes appears in the back garden. He's only visible for a little while then fades away. They may not have seen him, but the exhausted runners would have known how he felt!

The 2012 medals quiz
As you've seen, loads of British competitors won medals at the London 2012 Olympics. Not only did Team GB's stars amass gold medals in 29 events, they also won a further 17 silver medals and 19 bronze!

Fittingly, then, let's end London 2012 Remembered with a quick quiz about medals and golden glory...

1. As usual the 2012 medals had an image of Nike, the Greek Goddess of victory, on the front. But what image did they have on the back to remind competitors that they'd won the medal in London?
a) The River Thames
b) Big Ben
c) Buckingham Palace

2. The London 2012 medals also had some words round the edge. What did they say?
a) The date and place
b) The event
c) The winner's name

3. All London 2012 medals came with a length of ribbon, so that the winner could have it dangling round their neck. What colour(s) were they?
a) Purple
b) Gold, Silver or Bronze
c) Red, White and Blue

4. When the final design of the medals for 2012 was settled, the smart outfits that Britain's competitors were going to wear also had to be changed. How?
a) Smaller hats
b) Wider collars
c) Bigger pockets

5. To celebrate every Team GB gold medal won during the London 2012 Olympics, Royal Mail did something special. What was it?
a) Issued a special stamp
b) Delivered a telegram from the Queen
c) Painted a post-box gold

Answers
1. a): It also carried the London Olympics' 2012 logo.
2. b) and **c)**: The medals all had "London 2012" on the front. Around the rim was engraved the competitor's event and their name.
3. a): Purple is the colour of royalty … and the athletes who won them felt like kings and queens!
4. c): The pockets had to be made bigger – and stronger. The medals measured 85mm across, were 7mm thick and, at 400g, were the heaviest Summer Olympics medals ever!

5. a) and **c)**: All gold-medal winners had a special stamp issued with their photograph on it – showing that they were first-class males and females! In addition, a red postbox in their home town was painted gold in their honour. Perhaps there's one near where you live? Check out the map on http:// www.goldpostboxes.com to see. Royal Mail has promised that the boxes will remain gold for ever, as a permanent reminder of the Glorious Games of London 2012!

FLAMING OLYMPICS

OLYMPICS

QUIZ BOOK

CONTENTS

INTRODUCTION

With hundreds of different sports, thousands of competitors and millions of spectators, the Olympic Games is definitely the biggest sporting event on the planet.

The Olympic Games are so special they've even got their own Latin motto – *Citius, Altius, Fortius* – meaning: *Faster, Higher, Stronger.*

Why do the Olympics have this motto? Is it because you have to be good at computer games to take part?

Is it because you have to be able to laze around all day?

Is it because you have to be a champion food-taster?

No, the motto was chosen because it describes what the Olympics Games are all about: sportsmen and sportswomen trying to do their best, whether they win or not. This is known as 'The Olympic Ideal'. It's the way it was when the Olympics first began – 3,000 years ago! Yes, what we now call the 'ancient' Olympics took place in Greece in 776 BC. They lasted until AD 394 when they were scrapped.

Why? Because competitors had forgotten all about the Olympic Ideal and were more concerned with dealing out bribes to help them win.

The Games stayed scrapped until a French aristocrat, Pierre de Coubertin, thought it was worth trying again. So began the 'modern' Olympics, which were held for the first time – again in Greece – in 1896. They've now lasted for over 100 years. Will they survive for a thousand? That's just about the only question in this book you won't find an answer to!

What you *will* find are...
• awesome athletics questions
• boggling boxing questions
• sensational cycling questions.

In fact, there are 300 questions (and answers) on just about every event that takes place in the Summer and Winter Olympics.

Will you be able to race through this quiz? Will you get a high score? Will your teachers be strong enough not to cry when they get the wrong answers – and you get the right ones?

There's only one way to find out. Let the Olympic Quiz Games begin!

OPENING CEREMONY

The first event at every Olympic Games isn't a sporting event at all. It's the opening ceremony – the spectacular event that officially gets the Games started. People scramble for tickets to be in the stadium to see it (even though, for the 2012 Games, each ticket cost up to £2012!) and millions throughout the world tune in to watch it on TV – which is odd. Why? Because the same things happen every time! Yes, the opening ceremony has become a tradition…

For the very first time

Here are ten Olympic traditions, each dating from a different Olympic Games. Each of the games held between 1896 and 1936 is represented except for 1916 (when the Olympics weren't held because of World War I). Sort the traditions into date order, with the oldest first.

1896, 1900, 1904, 1908, 1912, 1920, 1924, 1928, 1932, 1936

1. Gold, silver and bronze medals for the first, second and third competitors in an event.
2. The Olympic flame, which burns throughout the Games.
3. The procession of competitors at the opening ceremony.
4. The Olympic flag with its white background and five interlocking rings coloured blue, black, red, yellow and green.
5. The torch relay, in which the Olympic flame is carried from Greece to the host country.
6. Teams representing different countries.

7. Women competitors.

8. The medal presentation podium, with its first, second and third positions.

9. The first separate Winter Olympics.

10. The first Olympics Games to take place outside Europe.

Answers:

1896 – 3. The procession of competitors. For the first-ever Games, this was more of a stroll than a procession. Nowadays, there's a strict order. Greece is always first, in recognition of being the country which began it all; then come the other teams, in alphabetical order. The host country comes last.

1900 – 7. Women competitors. All 19 of them!

1904 – 10. Outside Europe, as in St Louis, USA. The Games weren't a great success because they were combined with a world fair and spread out over a period of five months!

1908 – 1. Gold, silver and bronze medals. In earlier games, only winners and runners-up received prizes. The winner got a silver medal, a certificate and an olive branch. The runner-up got a copper medal and a sprig of laurel.

1912 – 6. Teams representing different countries. Before this competitors entered as individuals.

1920 – 4. The Olympic flag. The five colours were chosen because, in 1920, at least one of them appeared in the flag of each country taking part.

1924 – 9. The first Winter Olympics. That is, the Winter Olympics became a totally separate event from what was now known as the Summer

Olympics. This isn't to say that 'winter' sports hadn't been seen before: figure-skating had been an Olympic event since 1908!

1928 – 2. The Olympic flame. Lit during the opening ceremony, the flame stays alight until the closing ceremony (unless the gas is cut off earlier!).

1932 – 8. The medal presentation podium. Until now, there'd usually been a simple one-level platform in front of the guest of honour. The athletes had gone to him (it always had been a him) to get their medals. Now, he was forced to shift himself and come to the athletes instead.

1936 – 5. The torch relay. It covered 3,000 km, with the torch being carried by 3,000 torchbearers running 1 km each.

Flaming Fact
Memorabilia from the Olympics are often sold off when the event is over. Following the Sydney 2000 Games, for example, you could have bid for one of two medal presentation podiums in an Internet auction. Starting price – £500!

WHY COULDN'T YOU HAVE BID FOR THE TORCH?

Torch truth

Sort out the fact from the fiction with these statements about Olympic-torch relays.

11. A total of 21,880 torchbearers were used in the Beijing 2008 Olympics, the highest number ever used. **True or False?**

12. The whole idea for the torch relay came from a fun relay race at the ancient Olympics in which teams had to pass on a flaming torch instead of a baton. **True or False?**

13. In 1956, an Italian named Guido Caroli had the honour of carrying the Olympic flame into the Olympic arena – but instead of running in, he fell over. **True or False?**

14. London 2012 torchbearers had to pay £199 if they wanted to keep their torch as a souvenir. **True or False?**

15. In 2000, the torch was plunged into water on its way round Australia – but the flame didn't go out! **True or False?**

16. In 1948, during its journey from Greece to London, the Olympic torch took a detour to visit Pierre de Coubertin's house. **True or False?**

17. The first Australian torchbearer to carry the 2000 Olympic flame was an athlete named Nova Peris Kneebone. **True or False?**

Answers:

11. False. The highest number to date is the 101,473 torchbearers used to carry the Olympic flame from Greece to Tokyo in 1964.

12. True. The race was called the lampadedromia (meaning – guess what? – torch race!). The first team home with the torch still alight won the race. Their prize? The honour of lighting the sacred Olympic flame.

13. False ... but nearly True! Guido was the final torchbearer at the Winter Games at Cortina d'Ampezzo in Italy – and was on skates. Unfortunately he didn't see a cable that had accidentally been left trailing across the rink. He hit the cable but, still clutching the torch, he recovered his footing and carried on.

14. True. They cost £495 to make though, so the torchbearers got a bargain. One sold hers in aid of charity for £150,000!

15. True. The flame's route through Australia took in the famous Great Barrier Reef Marine Park off the north Queensland coast. There it travelled under water, staying alight because it was fitted with a specially invented underwater flare.

16. False. It was taken to the Olympic founder's grave in Lausanne, Switzerland. The real reason for the detour, though, was to avoid taking it through Germany (the straight route from Greece to London). World War II hadn't long ended and Germany had been banned from taking part in the Games.

17. True. Nova Kneebone, an Aboriginal athlete, received the honour because the 100-day journey round Australia began in the Aboriginal lands at Uluru-Kata Tjuta National Park.

Now, nearly – and never!

Olympic sports and events are a bit like pop songs. Some are classics that seem like they've always been around and always will be. Others are popular for a while, then fade away – and then there are those that get nowhere near the charts because even the cat can't stand the noise!

In each of the following groups of three events...
- one is in the Olympics **NOW**
- one **NEARLY** made it, but was thrown out after a while
- and the third has **NEVER** been an Olympic event.

Sort out which is which.

18.
a) Rope-climbing.
b) Rhythmic gymnastics.
c) Lasso-spinning.

19.
a) Cricket.
b) Snooker.
c) Tennis.

20.
a) White-water canoeing.
b) Waterskiing.
c) Motorboat racing.

21.
a) Women's croquet.
b) Women's football.
c) Women's karate.

22.
a) Skeet shooting.
b) Tin-can shooting.
c) Live-pigeon shooting.

23.
a) Arm-wrestling.
b) Super-heavyweight weightlifting.
c) Tug-of-war.

24.
a) Darts.
b) Beach Volleyball.
c) Baseball.

25.
a) Water ballet.
b) Bomb-diving.
c) Underwater swimming.

Answers:

18. NOW: b) Rhythmic gymnastics – a women's-only event featuring gymnasts jumping through hoops and doing somersaults while they twirl ribbons. **NEARLY: a)** Rope-climbing was an on-and-off event in Olympic gymnastics until 1932. **NEVER: c)** Lasso-spinning.

19. NOW: c) Tennis. **NEARLY: a)** Cricket, which was bowled out after its only appearance in 1900. **NEVER: b)** Snooker.

20. NOW: a) White-water canoeing (also known

as the canoe slalom).
NEARLY: c) Motorboat racing, which made its only appearance in 1908 before being sunk. **NEVER: b)** Waterskiing.

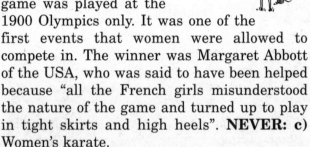

CROQUET NOT CROCHET!

21. NOW: b) Women's football. **NEARLY: a)** Women's croquet. The game was played at the 1900 Olympics only. It was one of the first events that women were allowed to compete in. The winner was Margaret Abbott of the USA, who was said to have been helped because "all the French girls misunderstood the nature of the game and turned up to play in tight skirts and high heels". **NEVER: c)** Women's karate.

22. NOW: a) Skeet shooting. A 'skeet' isn't a thing, it's a type of competition. The shooter has to hit 'clay pigeons', which are catapulted from side to side and at different heights. **NEARLY: c)** Live-pigeon shooting. Sorry, this really was an event in 1900. Even worse, the Belgian winner, Leon de Lunden, hit 21 of them. **NEVER: b)** Tin-can shooting.

23. NOW: b) Super-heavyweight weightlifting. The 'super-heavyweight' refers to the weight of the competitor, not how much they lift! Super-heavies weigh in at over 105 kg! **NEARLY: c)** Tug-of-war. This was an athletics event until 1920. It was then tugged out of the Games and hasn't returned. **NEVER: a)** Arm-wrestling.

24. NOW: b) Beach Volleyball. **NEARLY: c)**

Baseball – which was pitched in from 1992 to 2008 but then hit out again. **NEVER: a)** Darts **25. NOW: a)** Water Ballet (which is what synchronized swimming was called when it was invented in Canada in the 1920q). **NEARLY: c)** Underwater swimming. This appeared – don't hold your breath – just once in 1900. The winner was Charles de Vendeville, from France, who swam an incredible 157 metres before coming up for air! **NEVER: b)** Bomb-diving.

Flaming Fact

Whatever your sport, if you weren't judged fit enough one month before the ancient Olympics were due to start then you weren't allowed to compete.

WATER PERFORMANCE

Strangely, water sports didn't feature in the ancient Olympics – strange, because swimming was an activity well known to many of the world's ancient civilizations. Julius Caesar, for instance, was famous for his swimming prowess.

The famous epic Greek poem, *The Odyssey*, mentions swimming as well. So why there's no record of any ancient Olympians' water-sport victories being splashed all over the ancient front pages is something of an unfathomable mystery.

The modern Olympics didn't hesitate to take the plunge, though, and watery events have been included ever since the Games were refloated in 1896. And now, just as the real thing starts with events called 'Aquatics', we're opening with a section about these sports too. Here's a quick question to get you started:

26. Which of these Olympic sports *isn't* included in

the 'Aquatics' category?
a) Diving.
b) Swimming.
c) Sailing.
d) Synchronized swimming.
e) Water polo.

Aquatics antics

Even though they're in the water, aquatics competitors don't always find life plain sailing! Match these performers with the problems they faced...

27. In 1936, Eleanor Holm (USA) was the reigning 100 m backstroke champion – but she wasn't allowed to compete after being found guilty of this. (clue: in the drink.)

a) Using an asthma inhaler.

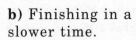

28. Ethelda Bleibtrey (USA) won three gold medals in world-record times at the 1920 Olympics – just one year after being arrested for this. (clue: she wasn't skinny, not really.)

b) Finishing in a slower time.

215

29. Greg Louganis of the USA won gold for springboard diving in 1988 – even after doing this. (clue: tough nut.)

c) Getting drunk on a boat.

30. Dawn Fraser (Australia) won the women's 100 m freestyle in 1956, 1960 and 1964 – after spending her childhood in this way. (clue: take a deep breath.)

d) Swimming in the nude.

31. Brazil's water polo team was disqualified in 1932 for doing this. (clue: too many peeps!)

e) Suffering from asthma

HAVE YOU EVER PLAYED WATER POLO BEFORE?

32. Greta Andersen (Denmark) had won the 1948 100 m freestyle but in the 400 m she found herself doing this. (clue: floating feeling.)

f) Winning more gold medals in one Games than the rest of the world!

33. In 1972 Rick DeMont (USA) won, then lost, the 400 m freestyle gold after doing this. (clue: take another deep breath.)

g) Hitting his head on a board.

34. A tight finish between John Devitt (Australia) and Lance Larson (USA) in the 1960 men's 100 m freestyle ended with Devitt winning gold – in spite of this. (clue: stop the clock!)

h) Fainting during the race.

35. At the 2008 Olympics, America's Michael Phelps set a record by doing this. (clue: gold rush.)

i) Insulting the referee.

Answers:

27. c) – not once, but often, during the American team's Atlantic voyage to the 1936 Games in Berlin, Germany. In her own defence, entertaining Eleanor – who was a rich lady – argued: "The team regulations tell us to use the same training methods on the voyage as we do at home. Well, at home I simply always have a glass or two of champagne after training!"

28. d) – but not during the Olympics! It had happened at a public beach ... when bold Bleibtrey had done nothing ruder than remove her stockings!

29. g) – the board in question being the diving board he'd just jumped from. Leaping high into the air and launching into a backwards somersault, the diver hit the board with the back of his head on his way down. It looked like he was destined to be Louganis the loser, but no. He completed the rest of his dives to become Greg the Golden.

30. e) – one of the reasons fantastic Fraser took up swimming was that she found the swimming pool atmosphere helped her breathe easier.

31. i) – they'd just lost 3-7 to Germany, the eventual silver-medallists. (No reason for calling the referee a big drip!)

32. h) – groggy Greta had to be helped from the pool. When the results were announced she'd sunk to the bottom!

33. a) – DeMont won the race but was stripped of the gold medal when it was discovered he had unknowingly used an asthma inhaler containing a banned drug. Raging Rick showed them what he could do the following year, winning the 400 m World Championship in the first-ever under-4-minute swim. (To this day, DeMont is still trying to clear his name and get his confiscated medal back from the International Olympic Committee.)

34. b) – in 1960, the judges' decision was what mattered, and they announced that Devitt had just beaten Larson ... only to learn that the electronic timing devices had made Larson 0.1 seconds faster! From then on, the judges' opinion was jettisoned and electronic times were used to decide the winners.

35. f) – magical Michael powered through the pool to win eight gold medals in the men's swimming. This was one more than the rest of the world's swimmers managed in the seven events he didn't win. With four more golds and two silvers in 2012, phantastic Phelps' total of 22 medals makes him the most successful Olympian ever

Plunging pairs

Here's a quiz that gives you two tests for the price of one – well, one sentence, anyway. Buried in each of the following invented sentences are two phrases related in some way to aquatic events. You may be looking for the names of competitors, of events – anything. The introduction to each sentence tells you exactly what sort of watery words you're after. Can you fish them out?

36. A pair of two-word swimming events from years gone by: "I don't fancy diving," said Walter Duck-Down. "All those rocks make it a dangerous dip; more of an obstacle course than a safe swim."

37. These are seen in Olympic swimming pools but made their first appearances 60 years apart: "During an amazing punch-up between high-board divers, relay swimmers and synchronized wimmers, judges had to leap into the water and act as lane dividers!"

38. The nicknames for two swimmers who took part in the Sydney 2000 Games: "Prize exhibits in the sea-life zoo are Sally the Shark, Eric the Eel, Paula the Porpoise, Oliver the Octopus and Willy the Whale."

39. Two locations used for Olympic swimming events: "The old White City Athletics Stadium was a lot closer to the River Thames than it was to either the Seine or the Amazon."

40. Two famous medal-winning swimmers: "Excited celebrity-spotters outside the VIP tent were rewarded by the appearances of the Duke of Hawaii, the Queen of Sheba, the Little Princess and the Lord of the Jungle."

Answers:
36. Fancy diving was the name given in 1908 to diving that involved somersaults and that sort of thing. (It's now just 'diving', of course). **Obstacle course** was an event that made its one appearance in 1900. It was a 200 m race in which the swimmers had to get over and under a row of upturned boats!
37. Synchronized swimmers made their first appearance at the Olympics in 1984. **Lane dividers**, running the length of the pool to keep swimmers apart, were first introduced

60 years previously, in 1924.

38. Eric the Eel was the name given to Eric Moussambani of Equatorial Guinea after he swam one of the slowest 100 m freestyles in Olympic history – and still won his heat! The other two swimmers in his heat had been disqualified and Eric had swum alone. **Paula the Porpoise** was the only other member of Equatorial Guinea's swimming team – and she swam even slower! By the time she'd finished her 50 m women's freestyle heat, the winner could have done another length. Paula had spent just six weeks training, in a river near her village.

39. White City Athletics Stadium – for the 1908 Games a 100 m pool was constructed alongside the athletics track (which itself was inside the cycling track!). The Seine was the 'pool' used for the swimming events in 1900.

40. Duke of Hawaii – the 100 m freestyle in 1912 was won by Duke Paoa Kahanamoku, a descendant of the Hawaiian king. He was representing the USA because Hawaii had become one of the US states in 1898. **Lord of the Jungle** – the winner of five swimming gold medals in 1924 and 1928, Johnny Weissmuller (USA) went on to star in more than a dozen films as Tarzan, Lord of the Jungle!

Flaming Fact

If you're a girl with a twin sister, then the best Olympic sport for you to take up is definitely synchronized swimming. In the pairs event at the 2000 Games four out of the 24 couples taking part were twins.

MINE SHOULD BE TEN MINUTES OLDER THAN HERS

Onboard or overboard

Try these teasers on Olympic events that involve 'boats' of different types – but don't scupper your chances of a good score by ignoring the clues hidden in the questions!

41. Which bubbly new event was taken on board in the Olympics of 1972?
a) White-water canoeing.
b) Windsurfing.

42. Rowers in the 1904 Games had to cover a distance of 1.5 miles – but what strange feature of the course really had them doubled up in pain while they were on board?
a) It was S-shaped.
b) It was U-shaped.

43. A Russian rower, Vyacheslav Ivanov, dropped something overboard at the 1956 Games – and it wasn't an 'oarsome' thing to do. What did he drop?
a) A medal.
b) An oar.

44. In 1900, a Dutch crew decided to replace something they'd had on board during a race – because they thought it was weighing them down. Was it:
a) A lifebuoy.
b) A live body.

45. Crown Prince Constantine of Greece, a yachting competitor at the 1960 Olympics, felt rather down after meeting his mother, Queen Frederika. Why?
a) He'd just won his race.
b) He'd just lost his race.

46. The weather caused Canadian sailor Lawrence Mimieux to stop racing when he was in with a good chance of a medal at the 1988 Olympics – even though the race took place in September, not on a May day. What had been the problem?
a) Strong winds.
b) No wind at all.

47. After their yacht broke down for the third time at the 1976 Olympics in Montreal, British yachtsmen Alan Warren and David Hunt had a spark of an idea about what to do about their craft. What?
a) Turn it into a powerboat.
b) Set fire to it.

48. After gunning his way to a fourth gold medal in 1996, exhausted British rower Steve (now Sir Steve) Redgrave announced live on TV: "Anybody who sees me go near a boat after this has permission to .... me!" What's the missing word?
a) Kiss.
b) Shoot.
c) Sink.
d) Board.

Answers:
41. a) White-water canoeing, in which competitors have to steer a canoe between posts while shooting the rapids! Windsurfing didn't make its first appearance until 1988 as a demonstration event.
42. b) The rowers had to make a turn so that they finished where they started. They couldn't have known whether they were coming or going!

43. a) The gold medal he'd just won for the single sculls event! Ivanov had thrown it up in excitement but failed to catch it before it sank to the bottom of Lake Wendouree in Australia. Water idiot!

44. b) It was the body of their cox (the person who steers the boat), who they'd decided was slowing them down because he was too heavy. Instead they recruited a young boy (not buoy!) from the watching crowd and with him on board they won the coxed pairs final by just 0.2 seconds!

45. a) The prince was a member of the Greek team that took the gold in the Dragon class yachting. Mum handed over his medal – then helped out with the traditional ducking for the winners.

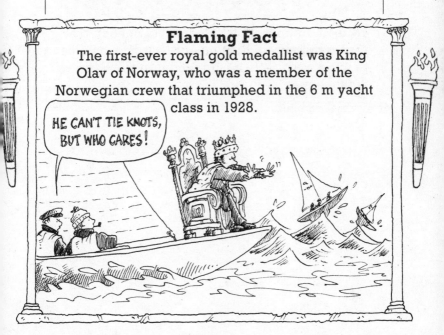

Flaming Fact
The first-ever royal gold medallist was King Olav of Norway, who was a member of the Norwegian crew that triumphed in the 6 m yacht class in 1928.

HE CAN'T TIE KNOTS, BUT WHO CARES!

46. a) The bad weather had caused havoc and two Singaporean sailors, in another race entirely, had been badly injured. Ignoring the fact that he was in second position in his own race, Mimieux went to their aid and stayed with them until they were rescued. It was later agreed that if anybody deserved a medal he did, and Lawrence the lifesaver was given a special award.

47. b) It gave a whole new meaning to the idea of an 'Olympic flame'!

48. b) Fortunately for Redgrave, nobody took him seriously – which meant that he was able to win a record fifth gold medal in the Sydney 2000 Games.

MARATHON MYSTERIES

Perhaps the most famous event at the Olympics is the marathon. It's so well known that the word has found its way into dictionaries. Check the one in your classroom. It probably says something like:

Marathon Any lengthy and difficult task (noun); requiring or displaying great powers of endurance (adjective).

You may think it's a good word to describe how you feel about doing your homework, but does that really compare to an Olympic marathon? It's a road race (even though it usually starts and finishes on the athletics track) run over the strange distance of 26 miles and 385 yards (42.2 km).

49. Who decided that the marathon should be this mysterious length?
a) An Italian count.
b) An English princess.
c) A French aristocrat.

Answer:
49. b) Princess Mary, when the Olympics were held in London in 1908, asked if the marathon could finish beneath the royal box at the White City stadium. This added another 385 yards to the planned 26-mile race ... and it's stayed that way ever since.

Finish or fail

That extra little bit of distance has proved to be a real problem for some runners. Sort out the tottering truth in this collection. Did the runners finish – or fail?

50. In that same year, 1908, Italian Dorando Pietri was presented with a cup instead of a medal. **Finish or Fail?**

51. It's 1948, again in London, and Etienne Gailly of Belgium was in the lead as he entered Wembley Stadium with only 385 yards to go. **Finish or Fail?**

52. In the 1912 marathon in Stockholm, the Japanese runner Shizo Kanakuri collapsed with heat exhaustion. He'd promised himself that he'd finish the race, though. **Finish or Fail?**

53. Another Japanese marathon runner, Kokichi Tsuburaya, was determined to win the race for his country when the Games were held in Tokyo in 1964. **Finish or Fail?**

54. In 1904, American Thomas Hicks was nearing the finish when somebody gave him some poison to drink. **Finish or Fail?**

55. During the first-ever modern marathon in 1896, Edwin Flack of Australia was kept supplied with drinks by his own bicycle-riding butler! **Finish or Fail?**

56. In 1972, the first runner into the stadium was Norbert Sudhous. Behind him, though, other runners were closing fast. Did Sudhous **Finish or Fail?**

57. Fred Lorz of the USA was first man out of the stadium at the start of the 1904 marathon – and first in again at the end of the race. Did he **Finish or Fail?**

Answers:

50. Fail. Pietri collapsed five times on the track (almost in front of the royal box!). He only managed to cross the finishing line with the help of the race starter, which was enough to get him disqualified. Queen Alexandra felt so sorry for Pietri (or embarrassed about her daughter's suggestion) that she awarded him his own cup as a consolation prize.

51. Finish – but only in third place. After 26 miles, he was overtaken by two other runners in the final 385 yards.

52. Finish (after Fail). Kanakuri dropped out of the 1912 race, but returned to the Olympic stadium in 1967 to run the final lap he'd missed all those years before. So his time for the race was 54 years, 8 months, 2 days, 32 minutes and 20.3 seconds!

53. Finish – but only in third place. Tsuburaya considered this a Fail and that he'd let his country down. He vowed to make up for it at the 1968 Olympics. When he got injured and realized he wouldn't be able to take part, he committed suicide. He left the saddest of messages: "Cannot run any more." There's now a charity in his name, the Tsuburaya Memorial Fund, which was set up to help runners anywhere in the world.

54. Finish – first! The poison was strychnine, which is only deadly if you take a lot of it. A little bit is helpful – which is why Hicks's coach gave it to him.

55. Fail. He couldn't even raise the energy to get on the butler's bike, he felt so tyred!

56. Fail – to the spectators' delight. Sudhous was a hoaxer who'd stripped down to his underwear just before the real runners arrived at the stadium, then ran round the track until the pursuing and red-faced security guards caught up with him.

57. Finish *and* **Fail** – because Lorz hadn't run the bit in the middle. After suffering from cramp, he'd stopped running, got a lift to the stadium, then started running again! Lorz didn't run much after that, though. He was banned for life.

The last gasp game

Running marathons leaves you pretty short of breath, so it's hard to say much. Even so, here are some things marathon runners have managed to say – except that some words have come out as GASP. Replace the GASPs by words from this list to find out what the runners really said.

boring, drink, faster, rejoice, wait, walk

58. The marathon race itself commemorates a run supposedly made by a Greek messenger called Pheidippides in 490 BC. He'd announced to everybody that their army had conquered the Persians by proclaiming: "GASP! We conquer!"

59. The 1952 marathon was won by Emil Zatopek of Czechoslovakia. He told a reporter afterwards: "The marathon really is a very GASP race."

60. In the same race, Zatopek turned to British runner Jim Peters, one of the favourites, and asked: "Don't you think we ought to go GASP?"

61. South Africans Christian Gitsham and Kenneth McArthur were leading the 1912 marathon when Gitsham said: "I must stop for a GASP."

62. Sportingly, McArthur replied: "I'll GASP for you."

63. Joan Benoit (USA) became the first-ever winner of the women's marathon, taking the 1984 Los Angeles gold. Afterwards, she talked about how it all began: "When I first started running I was so embarrassed I'd GASP when cars passed me."

Answers:
58. "REJOICE! We conquer!" They were also Pheidippides' last words, because after gasping them he collapsed and died. Why? Because he'd run from the Plain of Marathon to Athens, a total distance of 280 km!
59. "The marathon really is a very BORING race." That could explain why Zatopek broke the then world record by six minutes – he was fed up and wanted to go home!
60. "Don't you think we ought to go FASTER?" said Zatopek, explaining tongue-in-

cheek (a clever trick while you're running!) that this was his first marathon.

61. **"I must stop for a DRINK,"** said Gitsham as they approached a refreshment point.

62. **"I'll WAIT for you,"** said McArthur – except that mean McArthur didn't. Instead, he quickly ran off again to win the race and leave gurgling Gitsham to take second place almost a minute behind.

63. **"When I first started running, I was so embarrassed I'd WALK when cars passed me,"** said bashful Benoit, adding, "I'd pretend I was looking at the flowers."

The tottering ten

The history of the marathon is littered with so many staggering tales it's not always easy to see which runner is going to stagger in the winner. See if you can do it. In this tottering ten there are five winners and five losers. But which are which?

64. At the marathon medal ceremony in 1936, he bowed his head in sorrow as the Japanese national anthem was played. **Winner or loser?**

65. In 1904, he ran in his own shoes and a pair of trousers with the legs cut off. **Winner or loser?**

66. Even before the women's marathon in 2004, Ethiopian Elfenesh Alemu was in the Guinness Book of Records. **Winner or loser?**

67. During the race in 1900, he was forced to ask a policeman which way to go. **Winner or loser?**

68. Five weeks before the 1964 marathon, he'd had a pain in the stomach. **Winner or loser?**

69. He had a pain in the stomach during the 1980 race. **Winner or loser?**

70. She was trapped in a department store while, outside, the 1984 marathon was starting. **Winner or loser?**

THIS ONE'S ALIVE!

71. During the 1904 race, he had to cope with having two pursuers on his tail. **Winner or loser?**

72. At the 1960 Games in Rome, he stopped well away from the athletics stadium and couldn't carry on.

73. In 1908, he celebrated with the glass of champagne he was offered. **Winner or loser?**

Answers:

64. Winner. Sohn Kee-Chung had been forced to run for Japan because his country (Korea) had been invaded by the Japanese. All was put right for him in 1988, though, when the Olympics were held in a now-independent South Korea. Sohn, then aged 76, carried the flame into the stadium, proudly wearing his Korean running vest.

65. Loser – but one of the most gallant ever. Feliz Carvajal had lost all his belongings on the way to America from Cuba and had to run in the clothes he'd left in. He came fourth!

66. Winner. But her record wasn't for running. It was for having the world's longest train (600 metres!) on her wedding dress!

67. Loser. Ernst Fast of Sweden came third – the policeman sent him the wrong way!

68. Winner. Ethiopian Abebe Bikila in 1964. Five weeks before the race he'd needed to have his appendix taken out.

69. Loser. This was the Finnish runner, Lasse Viren, who then had to dive behind some bushes for a poo. It didn't help, though, and the rest of Viren dropped out of the race soon after.

70. Winner. Joan Benoit, the 1984 women's champion, used to have this nightmare.

71. Loser. In the 1904 marathon in St Louis, Len Tau, one of the first two Africans to compete at the Olympics, was chased a mile off course by two dogs. He still managed to finish ninth – so you have to admit that Len was a really dogged competitor!

STRANGE WAY OF TAKING YOUR DOGS FOR A WALK!

72. Winner. Abebe Bikila (him again!) came to a halt well away from the stadium because – unusually – the 1960 race started on Rome's Capitoline Hill and ended at the Arch of Constantine, both outside the stadium.

73. Loser. Unfortunately, it was during the race that Charles Hefferon of South Africa was leading. It made him feel all woozy and he ended up finishing second!

ON TRACK

Out of all the many sporting events, running track athletics is probably the one most associated with the Olympic Games. This should be no surprise. In the ancient Games a foot race was the first-ever event to take place.

So, as it all started on the track, having a quiz about starts and tracks is the obvious way to begin this section!

Start here

74. At the ancient Olympics, the shortest-distance foot race was called the 'stade'. About how far did the athletes have to run?

a) 100 m.
b) 200 m.
c) 400 m.

75. How far was one lap of the track at the 1896 Olympics in Athens?

a) 333.33 m.
b) 444.44 m.
c) 555.55 m.

76. How many bends did the 200 m runners have to negotiate in 1904?

a) None.
b) One.
c) Two.

77. When Britain's Eric Liddell won the 400 m in 1924, his world-record time wasn't officially recognized because of the track. What was wrong with it?

a) Wrong shape.
b) Wrong surface.
c) Wrong length.

78. The runners' lanes for the 100 m in London in 1908 were made from – what?
a) Paint.
b) String.
c) Canes.

79. The track caused a big punch-up in 1908 during a 400 m race. What didn't it have?

STARTING BLOCKS | RUNNERS' LANES | A FINISHING LINE

80. What was the starter's first job at the ancient Olympics?
a) To shout.
b) To point.
c) To scratch.

81. At the start of one of the 100 m heats at the 1896 Games, Danish sprinter Eugen Schmidt was helped by leaning on two – what?
a) Sticks.
b) Officials.
c) Blocks.

82. False starts have always been frowned on. What happened to a runner who committed one at the ancient Games?
a) He was disqualified.
b) He was stripped naked.
c) He was flogged.

83. What punishment was dished out to runners who committed a false start at the 1904 Olympics?
a) They were disqualified.
b) They were sent away.
c) They were forgiven.

84. How many false starts did 100 m champion Ralph Craig (USA) make in 1912?
a) One.
b) Two.
c) Three.

Answers:
74. b) – 192.27 m to be precise. The stade was a straight race down the length of the arena (which is why it became known as the 'stadium').
75. a) – it was also modelled on the track of the ancient Games stadium, being long and thin, with two very sharp turns at either end. The Olympics weren't held on a 400 m track until 1920.
76. a) – in 1904, the 200 m was held on a special straight section of track.
77. c) – by then, 400 m running tracks had become standard, but the track in Paris was 500 m in length. This meant that in covering 400 m, Liddell had only had to go round one

bend instead of two. As running a bend usually takes longer, his record wasn't allowed.

78. b) and **c)** – lengths of string were stretched between canes stuck in the surface of the track.

79. b) – the made-up lanes weren't used for other races. So when, in the 400 m, Wyndham Halswelle was trying to overtake his rival, American John Carpenter, there was nothing to stop Carpenter from moving out to block his way – which he apparently did! A rerun was ordered, but Carpenter and the other two qualifiers (also Americans) refused to run, giving Halswelle the only Olympic walkover in a running race! After that, all tracks were given lanes.

80. c) – the starter would scratch a line in the earth of the track for all the runners to stand behind. It's where we get our saying: to start from scratch!

81. a) – starting blocks hadn't been invented. Some sprinters stood up, some knelt down. Schmidt did a bit of both. He leaned on two sticks about 10 cm long, leaving them behind when he started running.

IF HE CAN DO IT, SO CAN I

82. a) and **c)**. He was **b)** already, because runners at the ancient Olympics performed in the nude.

Flaming fact

Apart from the danger of being flogged for a false start, runners at the ancient Games had to cope with a harsh rule at the other end of the track. Unlike the modern Olympics, a dead heat didn't give both athletes equal first place. Instead, neither of them won. The race was declared not to have a winner.

IF WE'RE EQUAL LAST, MAYBE THEY'LL SAY THE RACE DIDN'T HAVE A LOSER!

83. b) They were sent away by about a metre for every false start they made – meaning they had to run further than everybody else. This was great for Archie Hahn (USA) in the 100 m final. His three opponents helped him win the race by all having false starts!

84. c) Nowadays it's one false start and you're off – the track!

Go, girls!

These days, the women's track programme is as extensive as the men's. But it wasn't always the case. In 1896, there were no women's track events at all.

The founder of the modern Olympics, French

aristocrat Pierre de Coubertin, had fixed ideas about the part ladies might play. He said: "Women have but one task, that of..."

85. How did the baron complete his sentence?
a) ... making the sandwiches.
b) ... polishing the medals.
c) ... crowning the winner with garlands.

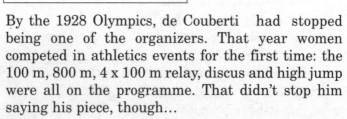

Answer:
85. c)

By the 1928 Olympics, de Couberti had stopped being one of the organizers. That year women competed in athletics events for the first time: the 100 m, 800 m, 4 x 100 m relay, discus and high jump were all on the programme. That didn't stop him saying his piece, though...

86. After the women's 800 m, de Coubertin complained that the tired women provided – what?
a) A very unedifying spectacle for the spectators.
b) Convincing proof that their legs weren't made for running.
c) Extremely poor value for money.

Answer:
86. a) After this, women weren't allowed to run races of more than 200 m ... until 1964.

What would Baron de Coubertin think if he were around today? This test will help you form your own opinion. Here are some of the current Olympic records for women. Decide how many of them would have won medals in the men's events in

1924 – the last Olympics of which de Coubertin was in charge. Answer gold, silver, bronze – or none.

	EVENT	WINNER	TIME
87	100m	FLORENCE GRIFFITHS-JOYNER (USA-1988)	10·62
88	200m	FLORENCE GRIFFITHS-JOYNER (USA-1988)	21·34
89	400m	MARIE-JOSE PEREC (FRANCE-1996)	48·25
90	800m	NADEZHDA OLIZARENKO (USSR-1980)	1:53·43
91	1500m	PAULA IVAN (ROMANIA-1988)	3:53·96
92	5000m	GABRIELA SZABO (ROMANIA-2000)	14:40·79
93	10000m	TIRUNESH DIBABA (ETHIOPIA-2008)	29:54·66
94	MARATHON	NAOKO TAKAHASHI (JAPAN-2000)	2:23:14
95	400m HURDLES	MELANIE WALKER (JAMAICA-2008)	52·64
96	4 x 100m RELAY	USA (2012)	40·82
97	4 x 400m RELAY	USSR (1988)	3:15·17

Answers:
87. Silver (Gold medal time – 10.6)
88. Gold! (Beating the 1924 winner's 21.6)
89. Silver (Gold medal time – 47.6)
90. None (Bronze medal time – 1:52.04)
91. Silver (Gold medal time – 3:53.6)
92. Bronze (Silver medal time – 14:31.4)
93. Gold! (Beating the 1924 time – and then world record – by nearly 30 seconds!)
94. Gold! (Beating the 1924 winner by over 18 minutes!)
95. Silver (Gold medal time – 52.6)
96. Gold! (Beating the 1924 time – and then world record – of 41.0 seconds!)
97. Gold! (Beating the 1924 time – and then world record – of 3:16.0)

Judging from these results, there's not much doubt that, if he was around today, belligerent Baron de Coubertin would become red-faced, embarrassed de Coubertin!

Last seen wearing

If you're not going to win your race, one way of getting noticed is to wear something eye-catching. Here's a selection of items that have been seen on Olympic tracks – except that the owners have become mixed up. Use the clues to return each item to the rightful athlete.

98. Boyd Gittens, running in a USA 100 m hurdles trial, didn't foresee the freak accident that caused him to lose one of the <u>long fingernails</u> he was wearing.

99. Paavo Nurmi of Finland had time on his hands when he ran the 10,000 m in 1952 carrying <u>his grandma</u>.

100. Michael Johnson (USA) stormed to first place in the 1996 200 m wearing his trademark <u>old golf cap</u>.

101. In 2000, women's 400 m champion Cathy Freeman (Australia) turned back the clock by copying an ancient Olympic tradition and wearing <u>nothing</u>.

102. Gail Devers (USA) clawed her way to 100 m wins in 1992 and 1996 wearing ten <u>running vests</u>.

103. Abebe Bikila of Ethiopia showed a clean pair of heels to the other marathon runners in 1960 by wearing <u>white shorts</u> on his feet.

104. In 1972, Dave Wottle of the USA had to head straight for a studio to apologize on TV for receiving his 800 m gold medal while still wearing his <u>kangaroo hide</u>.

105. The Jamaican 4 x 100 m relay team runners were almost counted out of their final in 1952. They only had three <u>contact lenses</u> between them.

106. The same applied to the American 3,000 m steeplechase runners in 1908. They were very short-tempered after being told that they would not be allowed to race until they swapped their <u>gold running shoes</u> for dark ones.

107. Felix Sanchez of the Dominican Republic, who became in 2012 the oldest runner ever to win the 400m hurdles, carried a picture of <u>a stopwatch</u> inside his running vest.

108. Australia's 1,500 m winner in 1960, Herb Elliott, bounded round the track in a pair of running shoes made from a <u>white sheet</u>.

109. Elliott's trainer, Percy Cerutty, was also kitted out. If Elliott was wide awake and running at the right speed, he'd agreed to wave <u>a suit with a helmet</u>.

Answers:
98. <u>contact lenses</u>. It was knocked out by a pigeon dropping! Boyd was given a rerun and qualified for the team.
99. <u>a stopwatch</u>. Nurmi did this in every race he ran, only throwing the watch infield when he started his final spurt for the finishing line.
100. <u>gold running shoes</u>. Johnson also broke the world record with an amazing 200 m time of 19.32 seconds.
101. <u>a suit with a helmet</u>. It wasn't quite

as they did it at the ancient Games, though. There, the soldier's race had the competitors carrying a shield and wearing a helmet – but the suits they were wearing were their birthday suits!

102. long fingernails. They were about 5 cm long! But the gallant Gail had 'claws' to be happy. Years before, she'd been so ill she was in danger of having one of her legs amputated.

103. nothing. Tough-toes Bikila ran all 26 miles and 385 yards barefooted.

104. old golf cap. Wottle was so used to wearing it to run in, he forgot to take it off for the medal ceremony.

105. running vests. Quick thinking led to a quick change between the first runner, Arthur Wint, and the fourth runner, George Rhoden – and a quick time. The Jamaicans broke the world record and won the gold!

106. white shorts. They were against the rules at that time because the judges thought they were harder to see.

107. his Grandma. After she'd died, sad Sanchez had promised to win a gold medal for her, so he carried her picture for inspiration.

108. kangaroo-hide. Obviously the kangaroo didn't bound fast enough, though.

109. white sheet. Cerutty did it – and was promptly arrested for trespassing on the track. Elliott won the race in a world-record time, then had to spend hours pleading for his coach to be released from the police station!

Flaming fact

The most obscure running accessory was probably that used by Forest Smithson in 1908. He showed his displeasure at the final of the 110 m hurdles being held on a Sunday by being pictured with a Bible in his left hand. Somebody was certainly on his side – Smithson won, in world-record time.

I THINK HE'S TAKING THIS PROTEST A BIT TOO FAR!

Against the odds

The Olympics are littered with tales of heroism. Here are just a few from the athletics track. But were the heroes victorious or defeated?

110. Joseph Guillemot of France was up against the great Paavo Nurmi in the 5,000 m of 1920 – but Guillemot was lucky to be running at all. He'd been gassed during the First World War in 1918 and had only taken up running to help his burned lungs. **Victorious or Defeated?**

111. Nurmi himself was faced with a severe challenge at the 1924 Olympics. After winning the gold medal in the 1,500 m he was out on the track again, just one hour later, for the 5,000 m final. **Victorious or Defeated?**

112. Michael Johnson (USA) was the hot favourite to win the 200 m at the 1992 Olympics – and then, just 12 days before the opening ceremony, he contracted food poisoning. **Victorious or Defeated?**

113. In 1952, Emil Zatopek was leading in the 10,000 m race when he suddenly wobbled, gasped and generally began to slow down. Soon the rest of the field had caught him up. **Victorious or Defeated?**

114. Dieudonne Kwizera had tried to get to the Olympics in both 1988 and 1992, but had not been allowed because his country, Burundi, didn't have an official Olympics organization. Finally, after putting lots of time and his own money into forming a committee, Kwizera made it on to the track for the 1,500 m in 1996. **Victorious or Defeated?**

CAN I CALL YOU BACK?

COMMITTEE PAPERS

115. In 1996, Venuste Niyangabo of Burundi had deliberately given up his place in the 1,500 m so that his teammate Kwizera could fulfil his ambition. Instead, Niyangabo competed in the 5,000 m – a distance he'd run only twice before. **Victorious or Defeated?**

Answers:

110. Victorious. Guillemot won gold, inflicting a rare defeat on Nurmi who said after the race: "Joseph ran with God at his side."

111. Victorious. Yes, just an hour after winning the 1,500 m Nurmi took gold in the 5,000 m too – in an Olympic-record time!

112. Defeated. Miserable Michael didn't recover quickly enough and was knocked out in the semi-finals (although he did win a gold medal with the USA 4 x 400 m relay team). He made up for it, though. After winning 54 straight finals at 400 m he won the 1996 race by 10 m – the biggest winning margin in Olympic history. Three days later, he won the 200 m in a world-record time. In 2000, he became the first-ever athlete to retain the 400 m title.

113. Victorious. Zatopek was famous for gamesmanship and he was only pretending. When the others caught up, he immediately raced off again to win the gold – and beat the world record by 42 seconds!

114. Defeated. Kwizera came nowhere – but when he finished he kissed the track in gratitude.

115. Victorious. Niyangabo nipped in to cause a major surprise and get the reward his generosity deserved.

Flaming Fact
The famous name of Nurmi featured amongst the gold medallists in 1936, too – for equestrianism. German rider Ludwig Stubbendorf's horse had been given the name of the star athlete.

IT LOOKS LIKE THIS RACE IS GOING TO BE RUN AT A GALLOP

Oops, scoops and bloops

Once upon a time, athletes were only expected to run or jump or throw. They would let their performances do the talking for them. All that's changed and now we're bombarded with quotes...

THE WINNER OF THE 100 QUOTES RACE IS...

So here's a three-section quiz about quotes in which you must work out what was really said by finding homes for these snippets:

backside, be the best, don't bother, hero to zero, Mickey Mouse, oarful, shifter, start shaving I guess, take away, too old

We'll start with things that athletes sometimes say, then wish they hadn't – as in the following blunders. Replace OOPS! by what was really said.

116. Said USA's star middle-distance runner Mary Decker Slaney: "What's the use of doing something if you don't try to OOPS!?"

117. Britain's 1,500 m runner, Steve Ovett, voicing his opinion of the ten-event decathlon in 1980, described it as: "Nine OOPS! events and a 1,500 metres."

118. Bob Matthias won the decathlon in 1948 he was aged just 17. When a reporter asked him how he planned to celebrate he replied "OOPS".

119. When the Dutch mother-of-two Fanny Blankers-Koen turned up at the London Olympics in 1948, the British team manager, Jack Crump, said: "She's OOPS! to win anything."

120. Said Canada's sprinter Ben Johnson when asked before the 1988 Games whether he'd prefer to win a gold medal or break the world record: "The gold medal. It's something they can't OOPS!"

Every newspaper tries to get a scoop by either printing a quote – or making something up. Replace SCOOP! by what was really printed:

121. After Ben Johnson's disqualification "From SCOOP! in 9.79 seconds."

122. In the 2004 women's eights rowing final Australian Sally Robbins simply stopped rowing, causing her team to come last. Next day the Sydney Daily Telegraph's headling read: "Simply SCOOP!"

123. When Ethopia's Miruts Yifter won both the 5,000 m and 10,000 m golds in 1980, the papers nicknamed him: "Yifter the SCOOP."

And, finally, some things are said which TV companies have to cover with a "bloop" before the programme can go out. Replace "BLOOP" in this pair of bad-tempered quotes from those who didn't win...

124. Mary Decker Slaney to Zola Budd, when the latter asked how she was after the two had collided in 1984, causing Mary to fail miserably: "BLOOP!"

125. USA sprinter Jackson Scholz, 100 m silver medallist in 1924, when asked years later for his memories of the man who'd beaten him, Britain's Harold Abrahams: "I remember his BLOOP!"

Answers:

116. be the best. Sadly Decker Slaney never proved it at an Olympics. She was injured in 1976, the USA boycotted the Games in Moscow in 1980 and when miserable Mary finally got on the track in 1984 she was in a collision and didn't finish the race.

117. Mickey Mouse. Embarassing, as the 1980 decathlon was won by his British teammate, Daley Thompson.

118. Start shaving, I guess. Four years later, and four years older, bum-fluff Bob won the decathlon again – and promptly retired from athletics!

119. too old. Blankers-Koen was 30, Crump was crazy. Flying Fanny won four gold medals in the 100 m, 200 m, 80 m hurdles and 4 x 100 m relay.

120. take away. But they did. Two days after Johnson broke the world record and won gold in the 100 m, he was found guilty of drug taking. He was stripped of both medal and record.

121. hero to zero. Referring to Johnson's world-record time, this graffito turned up on a wall in the athlete's village before finding its way into the papers.

122. Oarful. Robbins herself was given the nickname, "Lay Down Sally".

123. Shifter. He'd ended both races with sizzling sprints.

124. Don't bother. Budd should have been grateful; at least Decker didn't deck her!

125. backside. Except that Scholz didn't say "backside".

HAVING A FIELD DAY

...And we're not talking about footballers who are playing in midfield or runners who are leading the field.

Field events at the Olympic Games involve throwing things, like the javelin and discus, and jumping as far or as high as possible (but not at the same time!). They are lumped together with track events and called Athletics.

Field events were amongst the competitions first seen in the ancient Olympics. Events like javelin-throwing came straight from the battlefield (so if you think that's why they're called 'field events' you could have a point, ho-ho!).

Five field firsts

There have been plenty of notable firsts at the modern Games too. See if you can pick the winners from this field...

126. Legend has it that the modern discus evolved from something first thrown at the earliest of the ancient Olympics. Was it:

127. Triple-jump winner James Brendan Connolly's leap of 13.71 m was enough to make him the first modern Olympic – what?
a) Field-event champion.
b) Champion from the USA.
c) Champion in any event.

128. In 1968, Dick Fosbury (USA) became the first person to flop in his event – which was what?
a) The high jump.
b) The javelin.
c) The pole vault.

129. In 1988, Russian pole vaulter Sergei Bubka won a gold medal and claimed an Olympic record for his first – what?
a) His first clear jump in the competition.
b) His first try at the pole vault.
c) The first time the pole vault had appeared at the Olympics.

130. Harold Osborn was the first athlete to win the high jump by – doing what?

RUNNING IN WITH HIS EYES SHUT

WEARING TROUSERS TO SAVE HIS KNEES

USING HIS HANDS TO PREVENT A FALL

126. b) This is known because of a boulder that has survived to this day. It's inscribed: "Bubon, son of Pholos, threw me over his head using one hand." Apart from a difference in shape, there's the small matter of weight, too. A modern men's discus weighs 2 kg; Bubon's boulder weighed in at 143.5 kg!

127. c) Connolly's event was the first competition decided at the 1896 Olympics – which means he was a) and b) as well. It was a triple victory in more ways than one!

128. a) Fosbury invented the head-first, go-over-backwards style that all high-jumpers use today – and won gold. His technique was immediately dubbed "the Fosbury Flop".

129. a) Sergei was so supreme in his event that, before it began, newspaper advertisements said: "air-traffic control have been alerted!" He didn't even bother to jump until virtually all the other competitors had dropped out – and then failed with his first two attempts. His one successful vault was enough to win him the gold medal.

130. c) The fall in question was that of the bar he was trying to clear! This was in 1924, when the high-jump bar balanced on pegs sticking out of the back of the side posts. Osborn had perfected a (then, quite legal) technique of pressing the bar against the nearest post so that it didn't fall off. After this, the practice was outlawed and the design of the posts changed to make sure it couldn't happen again.

Jesse, Luz – and angry Adolf

The 1936 Olympics took place in Germany's capital, Berlin. This section describes what happened in one particular event. Using the words below, fill in the gaps to complete the moving story.

100, black, favourite, long, marker, no-jumps, qualified, races, long, record, relay, second, three, world

Jesse Owens was a fantastic athlete. In one afternoon at a meeting in the USA, he had broken **(131.)** .... world records and equalled a fourth. He travelled to the 1936 Olympics as a hot **(132.)** .... to win gold medals in each of his events: the **(133.)** .... metres, the 200 metres and the **(134.)** .... jump. But Adolf Hitler, the German dictator, was desperate to use the Olympic Games to prove his theory that some **(135.)** .... were superior to others. He'd made it clear to one of his country's athletes, long-jumper Luz **(136.)** .... that he had to beat Jesse Owens. This wasn't because Owens was the holder of the **(137.)** .... record, but simply because he was **(138.)** .... But when the qualifying event began, Owens hit trouble. His first two attempts were **(139.)** .... One more and he would be eliminated. That was when Luz told Owens that his **(140.)** .... was too far forward. Owens moved it back – and **(141.)** .... for the final. There he not only won the gold medal, but broke the world **(142.)** .... again. As for Luz Long, he came **(143.)** .... Jesse Owens went on to win his three individual gold medals – plus a fourth when USA won the 100 metres **(144.)** ....

Answers:
131. three
132. favourite
133. 100
134. long
135. races
136. Long
137. world
138. black
139. no-jumps
140. marker
141. qualified
142. record
143. second
144. relay

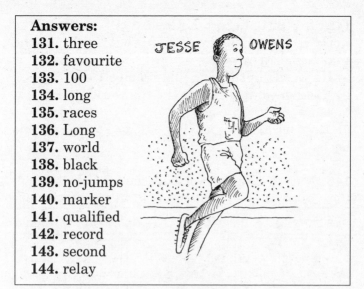

JESSE OWENS

Flaming Fact

After the 1936 Olympics were over...

• Luz Long died fighting bravely in the Second World War, which Hitler started; Hitler committed suicide rather than be captured.

• Jesse Owens carried on running and spent a lot of his time arranging sports meetings for under-privileged children. He died in 1980, aged 66.

• In 1984, the street leading to the Olympic Stadium in Berlin was renamed Jesse Owens Strasse. There are no streets in Germany named after Adolf Hitler.

Dafter, lower, straighter

Sometimes you'd be forgiven for thinking that the Olympic motto of Faster, Higher, Stronger should be changed for the field events. Here's a selection of incidents to illustrate why. Pick the correct answer – if you can!

145. In 1924, Robert LeGendre (USA) broke the world record for the long jump – but didn't win the gold medal. Why not?

a) He wasn't in the long-jump competition.

b) Another jumper also broke the world record, but by more.

c) He was disqualified for having springs on his heels.

146. Natasa Urbancic of Yugoslavia pulled out all the stops with her final throw in the 1972 women's javelin final – and just missed ... what?

A PIGEON   A PHOTOGRAPHER   A MEDAL

147. Robert Garrett (USA), the reigning Olympic champion, launched his discus in spectacular fashion in 1900. Where?

a) Out of the stadium.

b) Into the crowd.

c) Back over his head.

148. In 2012 not only did Germany's Robert Harting win the discus gold medal, he also showed his ability at another event. What was it?

a) Long jump

b) Javelin

c) Hurdles

149. Another group of athletes had trouble with their feet in 1908. A team from Great Britain successfully competed in – what sort of footwear?

| a) POLICEMEN'S BOOTS | b) DIVING BOOTS | c) WELLINGTON BOOTS |

150. Harold Abrahams had been selected to compete for Britain in the 1924 long jump – but he wanted to concentrate on his main event, the 100 m. So artful Abrahams put pen to paper and wrote – what?

a) A sick note.

b) A protest letter.

c) A ransom note.

151. In 2008 Brazilian pole vaulter Fabiana Murer discovered that an official had mistakenly removed the pole she'd been using. What did furious Fabiana do next?

a) Refuse to jump until the pole was found.

b) Jump on the official who'd lost it.

c) Stop anybody else from jumping again.

152. When javelin-thrower Sue Platt of Great Britain launched a stupendous throw in the 1960 competition she could not contain her delight. What did she do?

a) Jump for joy.

b) Sing the national anthem.

c) Dance the can-can.

153. After qualifying for the 1900 long-jump final, Myer Prinstein (USA) managed to get second place in a unique way – how?

ⓐ BY NOT JUMPING AT ALL

ⓑ BY HOPPING DOWN THE RUNWAY

ⓒ BY LANDING ON HIS HANDS

154. In 1912, Finland's Armas Taipale did it with his right and with his left, winning gold both times. Patrick McDonald (USA), though, didn't do as well and had to settle for gold and silver. What were they using?
a) Their eyes.
b) Their hands.
c) Their feet.

155. Jules Noel, from France, had really bad luck in the 1932 discus final. He'd just let go the furthest throw of the competition only to be told to take it again. Why?
a) The judges hadn't been watching.
b) He'd used a ladies' discus.
c) His throw had landed in the high-jump pit.

Answers:
145. a) LeGendre was competing in the five-event pentathlon. He came third overall even though William Hubbard (USA) made a long-jump leap that was 32 cm shorter.

262

146. b) The photographer wasn't watching, and almost got a really close close-up of a zooming javelin. Answer c) also applies; Natasa finished fifth.

147. b) Not once, not twice, but with all three throws!

148. c) As part of his victory lap, happy Harting leapt over a row a women's hurdles already laid out on the track. In other words, he leapt for joy!

149. a) The victorious British tug-of-war team were all London policemen. Their everyday working boots helped them to get a really firm grip on the gold!

150. b) The letter (which he didn't sign) said how stupid it was to pick him for the long jump, when he should be concentrating on the 100 m. Abrahams then showed it to the people in charge of team selection and suggested they left him out. They did – and hurtling Harold went on to win the 100 m.

151. a) and c) Mad Murer refused to budge from the runway until her pole was found. Then, when it was, she failed to clear her next three jumps and was eliminated!

152. a) Unfortunately, it was during the competition. Plonker Platt, after launching a throw good enough to put her in second place, jumped for joy so much that she stepped over the line throwers mustn't cross and the throw was disallowed. Try as she might sad Sue couldn't produce another one as good, and ended up in fourth spot.

153. a) Prinstein wouldn't take part because the final round was held on a Sunday. But in 1900 qualifying round jumps counted – and his qualifying leap won him second place.

154. b) At the 1912 Olympics, there were both single- and two-handed versions of the shot, discus and javelin competitions (two-handed meant throwing first with one hand, then the other, and adding together the distances). Taipale won gold in both for the discus; McDonald won gold for single-handed shot throwing but could only manage silver in the two-handed competition.

155. a) They'd all been watching (and discus-ing!) an obviously more interesting pole-vault competition. Noel's extra throw was nothing like as good and he only ended up in fourth place.

Quirky quotes

You've just finished your race and you're exhausted. All you want to do is crawl off the track and back to the changing room. What happens instead? A reporter starts asking you questions! So it wouldn't be surprising if you got all your words mixed up –

like in the five quotes below. Put the underlined words back into the speakers' mouths the way they really came out!

156. Jesse Owens, triple Olympic champion in 1936: "I let my <u>time</u> spend as little time on the <u>birthday</u> as possible."

157. Fatima Whitbread, powerful British woman javelin thrower, who came third in 1984 and second in 1988: "People think of me as the incredible <u>King</u>."

158. Tessa Sanderson, from Britain, who won the gold for the javelin in 1984 after failing to qualify in 1980: "In 1980 I was frightened to death of the <u>ground</u> but I took it like a <u>hulk</u> and came back."

159. When Michael Johnson (USA) won 200 m gold in 1996 with a world record time of 19.32 seconds, opponent Ate Bolden exclaimed: "19.32? That's not a <u>competition</u>, it sounds like my dad's <u>feet</u>!

160. After being praised by King Gustav of Sweden in 1912, decathlon winner Jim Thorpe simply replied, "Thanks, <u>man</u>."

Answers:

156. "I let my feet spend as little time on the ground as possible," was Owens' explanation of how he ran so fast down the long-jump runway and track.

157. "People think of me as the incredible hulk," said muscle-girl Fatima.

158. "In 1980 I was frightened to death of the competition but I took it like a man and came back." Tessa Sanderson, getting a little confused.

159. So amazed was Bolden that he said, "19.32? That's not a time, it sounds like my dad's birthday!" Johnson's record was so special that it stood for 12 years until Usain 'Lightning' Bolt beat it when storming to victory at the 2008 Olympics.

160. "Thanks, King!" "Your Majesty" might have been better, but nobody could say that Thorpe was wrong!

A RIGHT FIGHT

The fighting sports – boxing, judo and wrestling – are an important part of the Olympic Games. Judo is a relatively new Olympic sport, but boxing and wrestling have been around since the ancient Olympics. In those days, the fighters didn't wear gloves. They didn't wear anything else, either. One of the rules at the ancient Games was that the athletes competed in the nude!

That rule no longer applies, but others do – like those for ensuring fair fights. It wouldn't be right if a skinny shrimp climbed into the ring and found himself being beaten up by a ten-tonne titanic. So to stop that happening, all the fighting sports divide competitors into different weight groups. That way, if they do get beaten up, at least it will be by somebody who weighs roughly the same as them.

Weigh to go!

Boxing has always used names for its weight groups. Not names like Stanley or Wilhemina, but ones like flyweight (in which the descriptive part 'fly' is used to say that a boxer in that weight group isn't very heavy at all!).

Here's the complete list of weight names – except that they've been written with clues instead of descriptive words. Can you work out what the actual names of the groups are?

161. Not dark, lift off the ground weight.
162. Winged creature of the order Diptera weight.
163. Small chicken weight.
164. Tickly thing weight.

165. Form of electromagnetic radiation weight.
166. Mucky wallow weight.
167. Bellybutton weight.
168. Not one or the other weight.
169. Weighs a lot weight.
170. Wonderful, dumb bodyguard weight.

Answers:
161. Light flyweight.
162. Flyweight.
163. Bantamweight.
164. Featherweight.
165. Lightweight.
166. Welterweight. (Boxing also has a wallow-in-ping-pong-balls weight – in other words, a light welterweight!)
167. Middleweight. (Boxing also has an illuminated-belly-button weight – yes, a light middleweight!)
168. Light heavyweight.
169. Heavyweight.
170. Super heavyweight.

Flaming Fact

Judo has its own silly names, like extra-lightweight, plus half-sizes in the lightweight, middleweight and heavyweight categories.

LOOK – I TOLD YOU I WAS HALF-HEAVYWEIGHT!

Ancient and modern

Boxing and wrestling are both sports that featured in the ancient Games. But surely things have changed since then? You don't find the same things happening in the modern Olympics, do you?

Here's where you discover whether boxing is foxing or wrestling too testing. Decide whether the incidents described in this list apply to the ancient Games or the modern Olympics.

171. A wrestling bout once lasted for 11 hours and 40 minutes. **Ancient or Modern?**

172. A dead boxer was declared the winner of his bout. **Ancient or Modern?**

173. After a boxer surprisingly won his bout, a number of judges were sacked. **Ancient or Modern?**

174. A boxer was found guilty of bribing an official, but was still allowed to remain the winner. **Ancient or Modern?**

175. A wrestler would signal the start of the entertainment by hitting a huge gong with a hammer. **Ancient or Modern?**

176. This champion boxer won a team contest with three other men – and it was fought out in the middle of winter! **Ancient or Modern?**

177. A boxer was declared the winner of his fight after his opponent's teeth marks were found on his bare chest. **Ancient or Modern?**

178. Another wrestler gained the upper hand in his bout by rubbing sand in his opponent's eyes. **Ancient or Modern?**

179. Six wins in a row becomes the record for an Olympic wrestling champion. **Ancient or Modern?**

180. A man with a slave's name became the most famous Olympic boxer of his time. **Ancient or Modern?**

Answers:

171. Modern. It happened in 1912, in a bout won by Martin Klein of Russia against Alfred Asikainen of Finland. Klein was so exhausted afterwards, he couldn't fight for the gold medal and had to accept silver.

172. Ancient. The rule was that if a fighter was killed then he'd be declared the winner, and his opponent banished from all future Olympics.

173. Modern. In 1988 in Seoul, a suspiciously high number of Korean boxers had scored wins. The suspensions came after local boxer, Park Si-Hun, was judged to have beaten Roy Jones (USA). Jones was later awarded a cup as the best boxer in the Games!

174. Ancient. It was a boxer named Eupolus, who bribed three opponents to let him win at the Games in 388 BC. That was the rule. Although bribery was punishable by a flogging, a fine or a ban from future Olympics (or all three!), the cheat still prospered by being allowed to remain the winner.

175. Modern. Kenneth Richmond (Great Britain), who won a heavyweight wrestling bronze medal in 1952, became even more well known as the muscle man who did the gong-bashing at the start of films made by the Rank Organisation.

THEY WANTED A BIG NAME TO DRUM UP BUSINESS

176. Modern. The boxer was Ed Eagan (USA), light-heavyweight winner in 1920. Twelve years later, in 1932, Eagan was a member of the USA's winning four-man bob team at the Winter Games in Lake Placid – making him the first man to win both Summer and Winter Olympic gold medals.

177. Modern. It happened in 1924 to the middleweight champion, Great Britain's Harry Mallin. After losing his bout against Roger Brousse of France, Mallin showed the judges his chest. They agreed that Brousse had bitten the Briton and he was disqualified.

178. Ancient. Nowadays, wrestling bouts take place on mats; rubbing one of those into your opponent's eyes isn't so easy!

179. Ancient. The record-holder was called Milo of Croton. He was reputed to be so strong that he could lift an ox!

180. Modern. Cassius Clay (USA) was the Olympic light-heavyweight champion in 1960. Saying that his name was inherited from a slave ancestor, he later changed it – and, as Muhammad Ali, became the most famous boxer ever.

Fighting talk

Judo and tae kwon do are the oldest newest Olympic fighting sports! Judo only made its first Olympic appearance in 1964, even though the word ju-do is found in Chinese writings of the first century. The Korean martial art of tae kwon do, which didn't become an Olympic event until 2000, is even older – dating back to 50 BC!

181. What does 'judo' mean?
a) The strong way.
b) The quick way.
c) The gentle way.

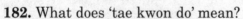

182. What does 'tae kwon do' mean?
a) The way of hands and feet.
b) The way of hands and eyes.
c) The way of eyes and feet.

Considering that they're supposed to be serene sports, judo and tae kwon do come with loads of gruesome talk! Do these scary seven terms apply to judo, tae kwon do ... or are they invented?

183

BODY DROP

184

SCORING AREA

185

CROSS ARMLOCK

186

INSIDES OUT

188

NAKED STRANGLE

187

SUDDEN DEATH

189

WATERY EYE

Answers:
183. Judo – it's a move in which a judoka (that's a judo contestant) throws his or her opponent over their outstretched leg.
184. Tae kwon do – the area of an opponent's face or body which a fighter is allowed to punch or kick to score a point.
185. Judo – in this, the poor victim finds a leg

around his neck and an arm being stretched at the same time.

186. Invented

187. Tae kwon do – no, it's not as bad as it sounds. If a three-round Olympic final ends in a tie, the two fighters go into a 'sudden death' fourth round, with the first to score a point being declared the winner.

188. Judo – a simple hold in which judokas choke their opponents by putting an arm round their neck from behind.

189. Invented

Flaming Fact

Fighters at the ancient Games got themselves fit by breaking rocks with a pick.

WHAT'S GOING ON?

HE'S BREAKING ROCKS. I'M PICKING 'EM!

SNATCHES AND SPLITS

Two sports that have been part of the Olympics since 1896 are weightlifting and gymnastics. You might think they're very different, but they've got a lot in common – and it's not simply that you can stay out of the rain when you watch them. Both require competitors to lift things. In weightlifting, it's a thing called a barbell, which has round heavy discs at each end; in gymnastics, the weight you have to swing over and around bits of equipment is yourself.

Three's a crowd

Here are some wicked weightlifting questions. In questions 190 – 193 you have to find the wrong answer, and in questions 194 – 197 the right answer!

190. Weightlifting in the 1896 Games had competitions for:
a) Two-arm lifts.
b) One-arm lifts.
c) No-arm lifts.

191. The weightlifting methods now used are called:
a) Snatch.
b) Grab.
c) Clean and jerk.

192. Lifting a weight above your head isn't enough. For any lift to be accepted by the judges, weightlifters also have to:

a) BE STANDING STILL

b) HAVE ONE LEG FORWARD AND THE OTHER BACK

c) HAVE THE WEIGHT STEADY

193. The animals which compare most closely to the heaviest weights ever lifted at the Olympics are:

GIRAFFE COW

ST BERNARD DOG

194. Competitors in weightlifting are themselves grouped by weight. The lowest weight group for men is:
a) 48 kg.
b) 56 kg.
c) 64 kg.

195. If two lifters manage to lift exactly the same weight, which of the two is declared the winner:
a) The lighter.
b) The heavier.
c) Neither of them.

196. Women's weightlifting events were first included in the Olympics in:
a) 1896.
b) 1960.
c) 2000.

197. The lowest weight group for women is:
a) 48 kg.
b) 56 kg.
c) 64 kg.

Answers:
190. c) – though the one-arm lifting event was quickly thrown out!

191. b) In the 'snatch', the lifter brings the bar to head height in one move. The 'clean and jerk' is done in two stages: first to shoulder level, in which the lifter squats, then to head height while the lifter stands up.

192. b) The lifter can only be in this position during their lift. If they don't then straighten up, the lift isn't allowed.

193. c) – it's far too light! Olympic competitions add together the total weight each lifter manages for both the snatch and the clean and jerk. At the Sydney 2000 Games, Hossein Rezazadeh lifted a world record of 472.5 kg – roughly the weight of both a cow and a giraffe!

194. b) The London 2012 champion at 56kg, Om Yun-chol of North Korea, lifted 168kg in the clean and jerk – that's three times his own body weight!

195. a) – because he/she has lifted more times their own body weight they're assumed to be stronger, even though they're not. Geddit?

196. c) – yes, they had to weight all that time!

197. a) The 2012 champion at 48kg, Wang Mingjuan of China, cleaned and jerked 114kg – nearly two and a half times her own body weight.

I CANNOT LIFT YOUR BODY WEIGHT..

Weight for it!

Weightlifting events have their fair share of drama, with competitors and spectators alike wondering what's going to happen next. Work out what did happen next on these occasions...

198. Charles Vinci (USA) found himself with a weight problem in 1956. With just 15 minutes to go before the weigh-in, chubby Charles checked and found he was 200 grams too heavy! What happened next?

199. In 1996, Ronny Weller of Germany had lifted a world-record total of 455 kg. Russian Andrey Chemerkin then stepped up for his final lift of the competition. What happened to Weller next?

200. Harold Sakata (USA), won a silver medal for weightlifting in 1948. What famously happened to him next? (Quite a lot next – like, 16 years later).

a) He did a dance.

b) He threw his hat in the air.

c) He sang a song.

In the gym

If any athletes have taken the Olympic motto to heart, it's those who compete in the gymnastics events. They try to go higher, faster and stronger all at the same time! There are three events:

• artistic gymnastics, in which gymnasts do things on bits of equipment like beams, bars and pommel horses

• rhythmic gymnastics, in which competitors do things with bits of equipment, like ribbons, clubs and hoops

279

• trampolining, in which gymnasts do moves and bounce at the same time.

There are a mind-bending number of names for the body-bending movements that gymnasts perform. But which of the following are real gymnastic moves and which aren't?

201. Cartwheel

202. Cat leap

203. Cross

204. Crunch

205. Double stagger

206. Flic-flac

207. Hitler

208. Leg circle

209. Reindeer

210. Snake

211. Splits

212. Tuck

Answers:

201. YES. A cartwheel is (according to the official Olympics description) "an acrobatic sideways roll with arms and legs extended". To you and me it's what you do when you're showing off in the playground!

202. YES. A cat leap means taking off from one foot, raising one knee then the other. Gymnasts score well if they do this purrfectly.

203. YES. Artistic gymnasts make a cross position on the 'rings' equipment – two rings hung from the roof. They have to stretch their arms sideways and hold themselves up straight, making a cross shape (and they get really cross if they can't do it).

204. NO. A crunch is an exercise movement for strengthening your stomach muscles.

205. NO – not quite. A double stag is a move in rhythmic gymnastics, though, with the legs split and both knees bent, while the back's kept straight. The aim is to look like a stag's antlers.

206. YES. With a flic-flac jump, the gymnast takes off from one or two feet, jumps backwards onto the hands and lands on the feet.

207. NO – but an Adolph is a trampoline move! It's a front somersault with three-and-a-half twists.

208. YES. It's an artistic move on a pommel horse. You keep your legs together and swing them in a full circle around the horse, lifting each hand in turn to let the legs pass.

209. NO – but a Rudolph is! On the trampoline, it's a front somersault with one-and-a-half twists.

210. YES. It's a move rhythmic gymnasts perform using a stick and ribbon. By waggling the stick in the right way they produce a rippling movement of the ribbon that looks like a snake slithering through the air.

211. YES. It's a position where one leg points forward and the other backward, at right angles to the body.

212. YES – but a gymnastic tuck is nothing to do with nibbling chocolate between goes. It's a move in which your knees and hips are bent and drawn into your chest, while your body is folded at the waist.

The flexible five

Use the clues to match these five golden gymnasts to their achievements.

213 RAYMOND BASS (USA)
CLUE: DIDN'T TIE HIMSELF IN KNOTS.

214 NADIA COMANECI (ROMANIA)
CLUE: A PERFECT PERFORMER.

215 LARISSA LATYNINA
CLUE: NEEDED A BIG CHEST.

216 CARL SCHUHMANN (GERMANY)
CLUE: FLEXIBLE FIGHTER.

217 KERRI STRUG (USA)
CLUE: STRUG WAS STRUGGLING.

OOOPS!

A PERFORMED A FINAL VAULT WITH A TWISTED ANKLE TO HELP HER TEAM TO A 1996 GOLD.

B IN 1932, WON THE LAST OLYMPIC ROPE-CLIMBING EVENT.

C WAS A GYMNASTICS CHAMPION IN 1896 - AND ALSO A CHAMPION IN WRESTLING.

D IN 1976, THE FIRST GYMNAST TO SCORE A PERFECT TEN DURING AN EVENT.

E WINNER OF NINE GOLD MEDALS IN THREE OLYMPICS.

FOUL!

Answers:

213. b) Raymond Bass won the final 10 m rope-climbing gold medal in a time of 6.7 seconds! When it came to climbing, Raymond knew the ropes!

214. d) Comaneci did this seven times on her way to three gold medals. She was 14 at the time, having been training since she was six years old.

215. e) Lithe Larissa's three Olympic appearances in 1956, 1960 and 1964, left her with 18 medals all told.

216. c) At the 1896 Games, sharp-moving Schuhmann won the horse-vaulting title and the wrestling.

217. a) Kerri Strug had twisted her ankle during her first vault and wouldn't have jumped again but for thinking (mistakenly as it turned out) that her USA team needed the points to win team gold. Courageous Kerry, ankle swathed in bandages, had to be carried to the podium by her coach to get her medal. Aah!

Finally, for all those of you who fancy being a gymnastics champion, a quick quote question:

218. Nadia Comaneci, golden girl of the 1976 Games, explained the reason for her success by saying: "I was ...., that's all." What's the missing word?
a) Gifted.
b) Lucky.
c) Grateful.
d) Pretty.

Answer:
218. a) Gifted, yes. Modest no.

Flaming Fact
In the early years of the Olympics, the gymnastics events weren't held in warm and cosy indoor arenas. They took place outdoors – in the grassy middle of the athletics track.

ROUND BUT NOT ROUNDERS

Ball games are incredibly popular throughout the world – but you won't always find them in the Summer Olympics. For example, softball (rounders for grown-up girls) and baseball were thrown out in 2012, going the same way as such games as cricket and croquet before them. Some sports, like snooker, pool and ten-pin bowling have never once been on the programme.

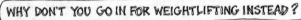

WHY DON'T YOU GO IN FOR WEIGHTLIFTING INSTEAD?

Sad, I know, but there's no point in bawling about it. There's still *plenty* of ball action to be found all around – as you'll see if you've got enough bounce to roll your way through this section.

True ... or bal-derdash?

'Balderdash' isn't a word that's used much nowadays. Well, it's time to change all that because balderdash means 'nonsense' – which makes it a perfect word for this quiz. Here are some Olympic ball game incidents. Can you sort out the truth from the balderdash?

219. In 1932, India won the gold medal for field hockey, with the USA taking the bronze – but there really wasn't much to choose between the two teams. **Truth or Balderdash?**

220. For the basketball event in 2008, extra-long stretchers were made in case of any of the players were injured and had to be carried off the court to be treated. **Truth or Balderdash?**

221. Reigning Olympic champion beach volleyball player Kerry Walsh (USA) won her first round match in Beijing in 2008 – and was given the gold after the game had ended. **Truth or Balderdash?**

222. Wimbledon champion Andre Agassi won the Olympic men's singles tennis title in 1996, following his father who'd done the same in 1948 and 1952. **Truth or Balderdash?**

223. Whiff-whaff became an Olympic ball sport in 1988. **Truth or Balderdash?**

224. A 1976 Olympic volleyball match between Canada and Czechoslovakia was halted because the crowd all stood up to watch. **Truth or Balderdash?**

225. USA won the first Olympic football title in 1996. **Truth or Balderdash?**

226. Women footballers at the Olympics can't be older than 23 and men can't be younger than 16. **Truth or Balderdash?**

227. At the Olympics, the USA have dominated a men's ball game that originally needed a helper on a ladder. **Truth or Balderdash?**

228. When the USA suffered their first defeat at this sport in 1972, time stood still. **Truth or Balderdash?**

Answers:

219. Balderdash. In their group match, India beat USA 24-1. They won Olympic gold every Games until 1960.

220. Truth. The stretchers were needed because basketball players are so tall. For example, China's Yao Ming (2.29 m) had a special bed made for him as well!

221. Truth. During the match Walsh lost her gold wedding ring in the sand. Afterwards a team of volunteers armed with metal detectors searched the court and found it again!

222. Balderdash. Mr Agassi Senior couldn't have played Olympic tennis in 1948 and 1952 because the sport was dropped from the Olympics in 1924, only returning in 1988. Andre's dad did compete in 1948 and 1952, though, as a boxer, for his country – Iran.

223. Truth. Whiff-whaff was one of the names by which table tennis was known in England in the 1890s.

224. Truth. Because they weren't watching the volleyball. They'd got to their feet because members of the Royal Family had just turned up.

225. Truth – but we're talking women's football here, which didn't reach the Olympics until 1996. Norway won the title in 2000, beating USA in the final.

226. Balderdash – it's the other way round. Men can be professionals but, apart from three permitted over-age players, they have to be under 23; women can be any age at all, so long as they're at least 16.

227. Truth. The game is basketball, which the USA won every year from its introduction in 1936 to their first defeat by Russia in 1972. When invented in 1891, peach baskets on poles were used as goalposts and a helper had to climb a ladder to retrieve the ball whenever a point was scored!

228. Truth – kind of. In the 1972 basketball final the USA was a point ahead of Russia with one second to go when the judges decided that the official clock was wrong. They had it put back by three seconds ... giving Russia enough time to score the winning basket.

Flaming Fact

Rugby Sevens is the only ball sport in the Olympics which uses an oval ball rather than a round one. It's said that it got its shape from the pig's bladders used to make rugby balls when the game was invented in the 1830s.

Sorting for size

If you've been going through life thinking a ball is just a ball, then think again! Every Olympic ball sport has its own rules about what makes a proper ball. The material it has to be made from, how high it must bounce, what it should weigh – they're all important. Oh, yes – and size matters of course.

Sort these sports balls in order of their legal maximum size, from the smallest ball upwards:

Basketball (men), basketball (women), beach volleyball, handball, hockey ball, indoor volleyball, table tennis ball, tennis ball, water polo ball.

290

Answers:

229. Table tennis ball, maximum circumference 12.57 cm – and it must be made of celluloid.

230. Tennis ball, 21.55 cm – and it must be yellow or white.

231. Hockey ball, 23.50 cm – and it must be hard!

232. Handball, 60 cm – (although a women's handball is 56 cm, because women have smaller hands!)

233. Indoor volleyball, 67 cm – and with a smoother outside than...

234. Beach volleyball, 68 cm – which is also less pumped-up.

235. Football, 71 cm – and it should weigh 410-450 grams at the start of the match (including advertisements and all the other pretty pictures).

236. Water polo ball, 71 cm (only 67 cm for women) and it must be, guess – waterproof!

237. Basketball (women), 72.4 cm – which is smaller than...

238. Basketball (men) 74.9 cm – but both should bounce between 1.2-1.4 metres if dropped on a solid wooden floor from a height of 1.8 metres.

Pretty technical stuff, eh? And you thought balls were just round objects!

Going for 'goal-d!'

The most popular ball sport in the world, Association Football (or soccer), was one of the first team sports included in the Olympic Games. The men's version made its debut in 1900 and – apart from 1932 in Los Angeles – has appeared at every Games since. Women's football was introduced in 1996.

So, who have been the star soccer squads in the Olympics? Find out with this football five-pack:

239. Three out of the first four Olympic football titles were won by which country?
a) Belgium.
b) Great Britain.
c) Canada.

240. Brazil, with five titles, has been the most successful country in the history of the professional football. But how many Olympic titles has Brazil won?
a) 0.
b) 1.
c) 5.

241. Hungary has won the Olympic title three times, on each occasion with a team made up mostly of – what?

242. Uruguay hosted, and won, the first-ever football World Cup in 1930. But how had Uruguay done in the 1928 Olympic Games?
a) They won gold.
b) They won silver.
c) They won bronze.

243. The same country won soccer medals in 1904, 1996, 2000, 2004, 2008 and 2012. Which one?
a) USA.
b) Cameroon.
c) Norway.

Answers:
239. b) A combined Great Britain team won in 1900, 1908 and 1912. Canada (true!) won in 1904 and Belgium in 1920.
240. a) Brazil's record at the Olympics is three silver, two bronze – no gold.
241. c) The majority of the team was in the Hungarian army – which made them 'amateur' footballers, even though they didn't do any soldiering and spent all their time playing!

YOU 'ORRIBLE LOSERS, YOU, GET PEELING THOSE POTATOES!

242. a) It was because they were reigning Olympic champions that Uruguay were chosen as the first World Cup hosts.

243. a) The USA men won silver in 1904 ... but in the five Olympics since women's football was introduced the USA's wonderful women have won gold in 1996, 2004, 2008 and again at London 2012 – plus a puny silver in 2000!. What would Baron de Coubertin have said?

RIDING RIDDLES

The two main events at the Olympics that are devoted to riders and saddles are cycling and horse riding (known as equestrianism).

Other events have had cycling or horse riding playing bit parts, though.

244. What are they?
a) Triathlon.
b) Modern pentathlon.
c) Gymnastics.
d) Athletics.

> **Answer:**
> **244. All of them!** a) Triathlon, introduced in 2000, involves cycling plus swimming and running. b) Modern pentathlon, first seen in 1912, involves horse riding plus shooting, fencing, swimming and running. c) In 1920, but never again, there was a vaulting event for horses. And ... d) Just once, in 1900, horses had their own Olympic high jump and long jump events!

Saddle up!

Horses have always been hard done by. The winners of the chariot race at the ancient Games didn't collect an award. Neither did the chariot-driver, for that matter – the laurel crown went to the horse's owner. And although it's now the rider who picks up the medals, the horse still leaves the arena empty-hoofed.

Is this fair? Try these questions to see how horses would get on if they were to compete against human athletes...

245. In 1900, the winning horse high jump was better than the winning human high jump. **True or False?**

246. The winning horse long jump that year was better than the winning human long jump. **True or False?**

Answers:

245. False. The horse, ridden by Dominique Gardères of France jumped 1.85 m but human Irving Baxter (USA) topped that with 1.90 m!

246. False. The horse, ridden by C. van Langhendonck of Belgium, leapt 6.10 m – only to be well out-jumped by Alvin Kraenzlein (USA) with 7.18 m.

---

247. In the 1900 human athletics, there was a standing long jump event, in which competitors didn't take a run up. That was won by Ray Ewry (USA) – and he out-jumped the horse too. **True or False?**

Pedal power

There have been cycling events of one kind or
another in each Olympics from 1896 to the present
day, though women didn't start competing in their
own events until 1984.

Cycling events come in three types nowadays:
road racing, track racing and mountain biking – and
they have lots of strange cycling terms to go
with them.

Use your own biking knowledge to match these
words to their definitions:

248 HIGHSIDE		ⓐ THE LOWEST GEAR.
249 ROCK DODGE		ⓑ ORIGINAL TERM FOR MOUNTAIN BIKING.
250 SNAKEBITE		ⓒ TO STEER THE HANDLEBARS QUICKLY TO ONE SIDE TO AVOID SMALL ROAD HAZARDS.
251 CARVE		ⓓ BEING THROWN FROM THE BICYCLE.
252 CLUNKING		ⓔ FLAT TYRE.
253 GRANNY GEAR		ⓕ TO MAKE A GROOVE IN THE TRACK BY SPINNING THE BACK TYRE.

Answers:

248. d) In particular, falling off one way while your bike turns a corner the other way!

249. c) A hard trick, but a lot harder if you don't manage it!

250. e) One caused by hitting something (like the kerb) so hard that the inner tube is pinched against the wheel's rim.

251. f) Usually a dirt track, not the pavement!

252. b) From the early days of the sport when mountain bikes as you know them didn't exist and riders would just take everything possible off their bikes to make them lighter (mudguards, brakes ... but not wheels) and clunk off across the countryside.

253. a) Because in this gear you need so little pedal power that even your granny could manage it!

Horse sense ... or bike brains?

Here are some real riding facts from the Olympics. But – are they connected to equestrian or cycling events? Do you have horse sense or bike brains? Select horse or cycle in each case.

254. This game of polo was a demonstration event at the 1908 Olympics. **Horse or Cycle?**

255. No medals were awarded in this 1932 team event because none of the teams had all their three riders complete the circuit. **Horse or Cycle?**

256. Lis Hartel of Denmark was an amazing and courageous woman. After suffering from polio, she won silver medals in her event in both 1952 and 1956. **Horse or Cycle?**

257. After suffering a badly broken arm, British competitor Virginia Holgate thought she'd never take part in her event again – until a vet cured her! **Horse or Cycle?**

258. This ride across country was introduced to the Olympics in 1996. **Horse or Cycle?**

259. There was a close finish in a 1936 event involving Robert Charpentier and Guy Lapebie (both from France). Charpentier was suspected of nobbling his rival by grabbing his shirt to slow him down. **Horse or Cycle?**

260. Although the 2008 Summer Games took place in Beijing, China, these events were held in Hong Kong. The reason? The stiff rules laid down for checking that parts were in full working order. **Horse or Cycle?**

261. After HRH Princess Anne rode for Great Britain at the 1976 Olympics – and had the world's cameras trained on her every move – she said: "This **Horse or Cycle?** is just about the only one who doesn't know I'm royal!"

262. The oldest woman competitor to date is Lorna Johnstone, who took part in an event at the age of 70 years and 5 days. **Horse or Cycle?**

Answers:

254. Cycle. The demonstration sport was bicycle polo ... but it never wheel-y caught on! Neither did horse-riding polo, for that matter, which was tossed out of the Olympics after 1936.

255. Horse. It happened in the showjumping, where the tough circuit prevented all the riders putting on a good show.

256. Horse. The illness had left Lis unable to move her legs from the knees down, so she had to be lifted on and off her horse. Her medals were won in the dressage event.

257. Horse. After a fall in 1976, Holgate's arm was broken in 23 places! Even when it had mended she couldn't ride properly. Then a vet studied her X-rays, gave her arm a good pull – and fixed it. A revitalized Virginia was able to saddle up and win a bronze medal in the 1984 Games.

258. Cycle. This was the year mountain biking joined the Olympics.

259. Cycle. A stewards' enquiry didn't change the result: Charpentier kept the gold medal.

260. Horse. There were better facilities in Hong Kong for enforcing the strict quarantine rules.

261. Horse – of course!

262. Horse. Lively Lorna was in the dressage event.

THE FROZEN OLYMPICS

If there's one feature of the modern Olympics that would have left ancient Olympians cold, it's the Winter Games – they competed in the nude, remember!

AND THE WINNER OF THE BIGGEST GOOSEPIMPLE EVENT IS...

The Winter Olympics are a completely modern invention. But how modern?

263. Did any of these events feature in the 1920 Olympic Games?
a) Figure skating.
b) Ice hockey.
c) Ski jumping.

> **Answer:**
> **263. a)** and **b)** **Figure skating**, in fact, had been in the Olympics since 1908.

As winter sports grew in popularity, it was decided to increase the number to include other events like ski jumping, speed skating and bobsledding. From 1924, there were two sets of Olympic Games – the Summer Games, which take place every four years, and the Winter Games which take place...

264. How often?

a) Every two years.

b) Every eight years.

c) Every four years.

Glacial and gone

When a city or town hosts the Winter Olympics, they're obviously hoping that they've thought of everything and missed nothing. It doesn't always work out that way, though. In this frozen five, the word MISSING plays a big part. Choose the missing item from these:

ice, skiers, snow, snow, sun

265. For the 1964 Winter Games in Innsbruck, Austrian troops had to be called in to deal with a problem of missing ....

266. The bobsled event at the 1988 Games in Calgary, Canada saw a spectacular crash featuring a team from a country better known for its ....

267. In 1980 there was plenty of white stuff on the ground in Lake Placid, USA, in spite of the fact that real .... was missing.

268. The bobsled course for the 1998 Games in Nagano, Japan, was designed so that nobody need worry about missing ....

269. In 1932, the 50 km skiing event wound through

a lonely stretch of woods and led to the unusual problem of missing ....

Answers:

265. snow. Innsbruck had had its mildest winter for years and the snow on the course had all melted. Austrian troops went into the mountains and brought down 25,000 tons of it.

266. sun! The team was from Jamaica, where snow has never fallen! Their exploits, which included pushing their sled over the finishing line after their crash, inspired a film called *Cool Runnings*.

267. snow again. No troops were called in this time, though. Instead the organizers spent $5 million (worth over $10 million today) on artificial snow. Unreal, or what!

268. ice. The bobsled course wasn't natural, but man-made. With computer-controlled coolant pipes beneath the surface, it was like a long refrigerator. All they had to do was fill it up with water and turn on the power!

269. skiers. The solitary stretch wasn't only closed to spectators – but also to race officials. When skiers weren't sure which way to go, they had nobody to ask. They just had to try and find their own way out!

Numbed numbers

The Olympics Quiz Book computer has got its digits in a twist and jumbled up the numbers in these frosty facts. Put the numbers back where they belong.

270. In 1924 at the first Winter Games in Chamonix, France, a bobsled team could number <u>0</u> men.

271. At Sochi 2014, the Canadian women's curling team brushed aside the opposition, losing <u>800</u> games.

272. An extra ski-jump competition was introduced in 1964. Jumpers could now enjoy throwing themselves off a hill <u>11</u> metres high.

273. In 1936 at Garmisch-Partenkirchen, Germany, the reigning champions – Canada – were stunned when they lost their ice-hockey title to Great Britain – especially as the winning team included <u>90</u> players who didn't live in Britain!

274. Norwegian figure skater Sonja Henie came last in her event in the 1924 Games. Understandable really, considering she was <u>four or five</u> years old.

275. Olympic regulations say that for the downhill-skiing events, the start point of a course has to be <u>54</u> metres higher than the finish.

276. Gold medallists Jane Torvill and Christopher Dean, from Britain, made history in 1984 by receiving the maximum possible <u>eight</u> points from the judges for the 'artistic impression' segment of their ice-dancing event.

Answers:
270. In 1924 a bobsled team could number <u>four or five</u> men. It was up to the team to decide.

271. The Canadian curlers won gold and set a record, losing 0 of the 11 matches they played.

272. In 1964, jumpers could enjoy throwing themselves off a hill 90 metres high. This was called 'the big hill' to differentiate it from 'the small hill' competition which involved jumping from a mere 70 metres in the air.

273. The 1936 British team included eight players who didn't live in Britain. They'd been born in Britain (which meant that they could play for them) but lived and played their ice hockey in ... Canada, the country they beat in the final!

274. At the 1924 Games, Sonja Henie was 11 years old. She made up for it, though, going on to win the event three Games running in 1928, 1932 and 1936.

275. For the downhill-skiing events the start point of a course has to be 800 metres higher than the finish. This was a problem for Sarajevo, Yugoslavia, when the Winter Olympics were held there in 1984. They had to build a special high-rise start line to meet the rules.

276. Torvill and Dean received the maximum possible 54 points – six points from each of the nine judges.

Arctic 'appenings

There have been some strange events seen at the Winter Olympics – but were they all to do with proper Olympic winter sports events? Judge for yourself. Were each of the following to do with real events, or non-events?

277. In 1994, spectators at the Winter Games in Lillehammer, Norway, saw a number of sleds being pulled across ice by teams of four-legged animals. **Event or Non-Event?**

278. In 1932, spectators at the Winter Games in Lake Placid, USA, saw a number of sleds being pulled across ice by teams of four-legged animals. **Event or Non-Event?**

279. At Chamonix in 1924, Charles Granville Bruce was awarded a medal for mountain climbing. **Event or Non-Event?**

280. At the 1994 Winter Games, Marc Gagnon (Canada) won a bronze medal for doing something faster than anybody else. **Event or Non-Event?**

281. People with numbers on their back and big

boots on their feet regularly took to the ice at the 1936 Winter Olympics. **Event or Non-Event?**

282. A boy/girl partnership named Hidy and Howdy featured heavily at Calgary, Canada in 1988. **Event or Non-Event?**

Answers:

277. Non-Event. The four-legged creatures were reindeer, and the spectators were watching a pageant during the opening ceremony.

278. Event. The four-legged creatures were dogs, and this was a dog-sled race. (As it was only included as a demonstration event, and has never been included as an official Olympic sport, Non-Event is a correct answer too!)

279. Non-Event. At the early Winter Games, honorary medals – called 'Merits for Alpinism' – were awarded to people who'd done something in snowy mountains. Charles Granville Bruce got his for being the leader of a 1922 expedition that attempted (and failed) to climb Mount Everest.

280. Event. The 1 km short track skating event, to be exact. Heats were used to find the fastest skaters for an 'A' final to decide gold and silver. The winner of a 'B' final would get the bronze medal. Gagnon felt great when he won the 'B' race, but turned into Mad Marc when he learned his time was faster than that of the gold and silver winners from the 'A' final!

281. Event. But if you thought it was ice hockey, be honest and deduct a point. The people were the judges for the figure-skating competition who would take to the ice in order to get a close-up view of the skaters during a section in which they had to skate some compulsory exercises.

282. Non-Event, but they did turn up at most events. Hidy and Howdy were the Games' polar bear mascots.

YOU ALWAYS HAVE TO SHOW OFF!

Polar problems

Just because the Winter Olympics take place in cold weather doesn't mean that there aren't plenty of heated arguments – as this collection of polar problems shows. They weren't as described here, though, because their causes have been mixed up. Rearrange the underlined words to show the true picture.

283. In 1932, Finnish world champion speed skater Clas Thunberg refused to start with other competitors because <u>they said her helmet was illegal</u>.

284. In 1964, slalom silver medallist Marielle Goitschel wanted to get her own back on the girl who'd won gold even though <u>she'd arranged for her to be beaten up</u>.

285. Many Austrian and Swiss competitors were banned from taking part in 1936 because <u>they weren't heavy enough</u>.

286. The 1952 four-man bobsled winners, Germany, only triumphed after realizing that <u>they were warming their runners before a race</u>.

287. In 2010, Britain's Amy Williams beat her rivals to win gold in the downhill skeleton event even though <u>they were hotel ski instructors</u>.

288. In 1968, three female East German competitors in the luge event (a luge is a kind of sliding tea-tray) were disqualified because <u>they were sisters</u>.

289. USA ice skater Nancy Kerrigan wouldn't have been blamed for totally freezing out teammate Tonya Harding in 1994 because <u>they weren't paired up</u>.

Answers:
283. Careful Clas refused to start with other competitors because <u>they weren't paired up</u>. The usual way of starting speed skating events was to send the skaters out in pairs to avoid collisions. When the organizers decided to scrap this and have a big scramble at the start Thunberg thumbed his nose at them and withdrew.

284. Marielle Goitschel wanted to get her own back on the girl who'd won gold even though <u>they were sisters</u>. Yes, it was her sister Christine who'd beaten her into second place. Marielle did it, too. In the giant slalom event she won gold – with Christine having to settle for silver.

285. Many Austrian and Swiss competitors were banned from taking part in 1936 because <u>they were hotel ski instructors</u>. Only amateurs were allowed to compete and because ski instructors were paid to teach gallumping guests, that ruled them out. It caused a holy hotel row because that was the job all the best skiers did when they weren't skiing.

286. Germany's four-man bob team only triumphed after realizing that <u>they weren't heavy enough</u>. Noticing how well heavyweight teams did in training runs, the Germans scrapped the two light squads they were going to enter and came up with one that was gargantuan enough to grab the gold.

287. Awesome Amy's rivals were overruled when <u>they said her helmet was illegal</u>. They'd argued that it gave her a speed advantage. Nut cases!

288. Three female East German luge competitors were disqualified because <u>they were warming their runners before a race</u>. Why did this trick get such a frosty reception? Because it was designed to help them to a faster time by melting bits of ice that would otherwise stick to their runners and slow them down).

289. Nancy Kerrigan wouldn't have been blamed for totally freezing out Tonya Harding because <u>she'd arranged for her to be beaten up</u>. It had happened at that year's USA Championships when somebody leapt out and clubbed Kerrigan in the leg, attempting to put her out of action completely. Harding was under investigation, but was allowed to compete in the Olympics where she came nowhere and a recovered Kerrigan earned silver. Later, though, she admitted she'd been involved and was banned from amateur skating.

Eddie Edwards

Eddie Edwards of Great Britain was a one-man polar problem. In 1988, funding himself and without any formal training, he turned up for the Olympic ski-jump competition. His equipment was so dodgy that other skiers had a whip-round to get him some proper skis. He competed in both 70 m and 90 m events – and came a long way last in both. But did he become famous?

Here are just a few of the things said about Eddie. Fill in the blanks using these words:

clowns, crazy, eagle, fly, loser, sportsman

290. Rob McCormack, official in charge of the ski-jump competition: "Eddie doesn't .... He just drops out of the sky. It's not ski-jumping."

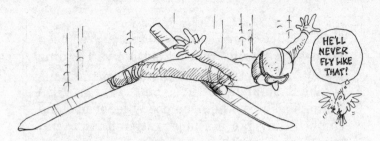

291. Finnish ski-jump star and gold medallist, Matti Nykanen: "You must not laugh at Eddie. He is good for our sport. We need some ...."

292. Julian Brand, a sports agent, explaining why Eddie became famous: "His appeal is because he is such a spectacular ...."

293. Everybody had their say about him, even darts player Eric Bristow: "Don't tell me he's a ....!"

294. At the closing ceremony, Eddie's nickname even got a mention in the President's closing speech: "At this Olympic Games some competitors have won gold and some have broken records, and one has even flown like an ...."

295. And what did Eddie himself say? "Everybody thinks I'm .... They're probably right."

Answers:
290. Fly.
291. Clowns.
292. Loser.
293. Sportsman. Bristow was trying to respond to criticism that darts wasn't a real sport.

294. Eagle.
295. Crazy.

But Eddie the Eagle had the last laugh. He became so well known that he made a small fortune from newspapers and TV when the Games were over. And he's still a star. When visitors to the Calgary site watch the commemorative video of the 1988 Winter Olympics, the longest slot they see is devoted to Eddie Edwards!

Flaming Fact
In the women's ice hockey at Sochi 2014, Florence Schelling (Switzerland) set a record for a goalkeeper with 252 saves out of 276 shots. But then fabulous Florence was used to setting records. Back home, she'd become the first woman to play in the Swiss Men's National League!

CLOSING CEREMONY

The Games are over. Soon it will be time to count your medals. But first, here are a final five questions. Will they help you on to the winner's podium?

Congratulations!

296. At the first modern Olympics in 1896, what did event winners receive?
a) A gold medal
b) A silver medal
c) A crown of olive leaves

297. What did those finishing second receive in 1896?
a) A silver medal
b) A bronze medal
c) A crown of laurel leaves

298. What did third-placed competitors receive in 1896?
a) A bronze medal
b) Nothing
c) A crown of oak leaves

299. The medals for Rio 2016 will contain gold, silver and bronze as usual. But as part of Rio 2016's aim to cut out unnecessary waste, the medals will also have mixed in with them recycled metal that's come from - where?
a) Broken-down cars
b) Electronics equipment
c) Children's bicycles

And lastly, a really easy question to finish with...

300. Medal-winners or not, every Olympic competitor is invited to the Closing Ceremony. They hear speeches, see demonstrations, watch the Olympic flame being extinguished ... and sing a national anthem – of which country?
(a) Greece
(b) The country hosting the Games
(c) The country due to host the Games in four years time.

Answers

296. b) and **c).** The olive leaves were a reminder of the prize given to winners at the ancient Olympics.
297. b) and **c)**
298. b). Bronze medals for third-placed competitors were first awarded in 1908.
299. b). So medal-winners could have bits of computers, radios or even refrigerators hanging round their necks!

300. a), **b)** and **c)**. All three anthems are played at the Closing Ceremony.

Medal table

So, how did you do? Did you sprint to the finish or treat it as a marathon? Did you shoot a high score or dive to a low one?

You've faced 300 questions altogether. So step up and receive your award!

If your score was pretty rubbish then all I can say is that it's a good time to remember the words that were first displayed at the 1932 Olympics and have been given pride of place ever since. Baron de Coubertin had heard them at a church service and liked them:

"The most important thing is not to win but to take part, just as the most important thing in life is not the triumph but the struggle. The essential thing is not to have conquered but to have fought well."

They're what the Olympics should be all about – no question!